Weekends Away
Without Leaving Home

The Ultimate
World Party
Theme Book

Foreword by

Nina Lesowitz and *Lara Morris Starr*

Conari Press
Berkeley, California

Conari Press books are distributed by Publishers Group West.

Cover Illustration and Design: Anne Smith
Book Design: Claudia Smelser
Layout and Composition: Jaime Robles

Library of Congress Cataloging-in-Publication Data

Weekends away without leaving home : the ultimate world party theme book
    p.   cm.
  ISBN 1–57324–761–8
  1. Cookery, International. 2. Entertaining. I. Conari Press.
TX725.A1 W365 2002
641.59—dc21   2001004358

Printed in Canada on recycled paper.
01 02 03 TC 10 9 8 7 6 5 4 3 2 1

Weekends Away
Without Leaving Home

Acknowledgments	v
Foreword	vii
Welcome to Armchair Adventures!	ix
Brazen in *Brazil*	1
A Fling Down *Mexico* Way	17
Kicking Up Your Heels in *Scotland*	33
Putting on the Green and the Guinness in *Ireland*	47
I'd Rather Be in *Paris*	61
Touring *Tuscany*	87
Glorious *Greece*	105
The Magic of *Morocco*	125
Into *Africa*	139
A Musical Wonderland in *St. Petersburg*	155
Passage to *India*	171
Fun and Feasting in *China*	189
Romance and Relaxation in *Thailand*	209
Journey to *Japan*	225
Idling in *Australia*	241
Index	264

Acknowledgments

This book was born at a brainstorming editorial retreat that Conari Press held with our whole staff. One idea led to another, but Production Manager Jenny Collins really birthed the concept by telling us about a weekend that one of her roommates, Suzanne Gooding, organized for a friend.

This has been truly a collective effort, with many folks from Conari pitching in to write chapters, including Jenny Collins, Mignon Freeman, Mary Jane Ryan, Will Glennon, Leslie Berriman, Brenda Knight, Sharon Donovan, Teresa Coronado, Julie Kessler, Rosie Levy, and Heather McArthur. Heather was the point person who pulled all the pieces together, while Mary Jane did the content editing and Pam Suwinsky the copyediting. In addition, we had invaluable help from Josh Merlin and Debbie Adler, Donald McIlraith, Genna Barfoot, Leah Russell, and Ofer Caspi. Thanks to everyone who played a part.

Foreword

by Nina Lesowitz and Lara Morris Starr,

authors of **The Party Girl Cookbook**

We've all been there. You've got a bad case of wanderlust, but the distance between your passport and your passbook won't allow for much more than a trip to the video store. The good news is, if you can stretch your budget to cover brief layovers at the market, library, and thrift shop, you've pretty much got yourself a first-class ticket to Partyville!

The very best parties have a solid theme that is carried out from invitation through party favors, and what better theme than a virtual trip to anywhere—or everywhere—in the world, played out over an entire weekend? You can entertain your entire entourage of friends, that one special companion, or take a solo flight of fantasy to the locale of your dreams.

The first stop on your itinerary is the proper state of mind. Approach your weekend as though you are truly preparing to travel. When your friends and co-workers ask you about your weekend plans, by all means mention that you are going to

Morocco or Japan. Either smile vaguely when they give you a quizzical look, or take the opportunity to explain what you're doing. Stop the newspaper and mail for a few days, and make a pledge to let the machine answer the phone.

You can use the tips in *Weekends Away Without Leaving Home* in a variety of ways: recreate a favorite vacation (wouldn't you just love a chance to haul out those old souvenirs and photo albums?), teach your kids about a new culture, research and share your heritage, or explore a region that's always interested you.

Select the movies, books, foods, and a couple of decorative flourishes that will recreate the sights, sounds, taste, and texture of anyplace you'd like to visit, for a fraction of the cost (and almost none of the hassle). With the editors of Conari Press as your tour guides, your living room can easily be transformed into a Mexican plaza, your dining room a Parisian café, your backyard the Australian outback. When you immerse yourself in the culture of a foreign country, you'll feel the cares of the work-a-day world slip away as though you truly are on vacation, and you'll emerge from your weekend enriched by a cultural experience and yet refreshed enough to bounce back into "real life."

All of this without long check-in lines, inoculations against exotic diseases, and hotels with questionable hygiene. Now that's what we call a *bon voyage!*

Welcome to Armchair Adventures!

A WEEKEND away! Who doesn't need such an experience every once in a while? A chance to leave your cares and busyness behind, to see new sights and taste new food, to bask in the ambiance of someplace different, to recharge your batteries and return renewed and refreshed.

But what if you're tired of all the places you can easily get to for a weekend, and your budget can't stretch to include a trip to an exotic locale? Or you are housebound for any number of reasons—small children, illness, out of vacation days at work . . . ?

Weekends Away Without Leaving Home to the rescue. Among these pages, you will find the makings for fifteen wonderful, rejuvenating weekends away—without ever leaving home or spending a wad of money! With help from this book, you can journey to cities and countries you've always dreamed of visiting, or re-experience the joy you felt when you *were* able to travel.

Weekends Away Without Leaving Home is based on a simple assumption: That with a tiny bit of ingenuity and effort on your part, you can create a wonderful weekend that brings almost as much pleasure as an actual vacation away—without the hassle of long flights, foreign currency exchange, or large credit card bills.

The editors at Conari Press have selected some of the premier travel destinations in the world for your enjoyment and offer ideas for creating an authentic experience in the comfort of your own backyard. Each chapter was written by someone who either has spent some time in the country or city featured, or has a close affinity to that locale, and reflects the unique sensibility of the author. You can choose a quiet weekend with classical music in St. Petersburg, for instance, or a wild *Carnaval* theme in Brazil. From organizing a weekend around a Chinese holiday to touring the Tuscan countryside, there is truly something for everyone here.

If you are attracted to a particular locale and the theme doesn't appeal, feel free to pick and choose the elements of the experience that do call to you. Reading the chapter on Ireland, for instance, inspired me to host a weekend party in which people read out loud to one another from the great Irish poets. But I steered clear of the Irish cuisine and opted for Italian instead.

You can design your weekend for a cozy *tête-a-tête* for two or plan on having a whole gang of friends—either for the entire time, *à la* pajama party, or perhaps for an afternoon or evening. And while we have structured each chapter around a weekend, you can easily use this book to create a theme for a dinner party or for an entire week by yourself.

No matter the place, the format of each chapter is the same. We first offer suggestions for setting the scene—both in terms of atmosphere and décor, and, in some cases, activities that you might want to indulge in to really get in the mood. Then we move to books that you might want to read, either before the weekend to get ideas for your adventure, or as part of the weekend itself. Suggestions for videos and music follow, and we end by suggesting a meal to prepare as well as cookbooks you might want to look at for other meals.

*P*utting a Weekend Together

Just as going away requires some planning and forethought, so do our weekends at home. The items we suggest in each category are readily available at thrift stores, libraries, used bookstores, and music and video rental shops. The idea is to make this as easy and low cost for you as possible. Feel free to let your imagination go wild, and substitute anything that appeals you.

The Internet is a treasure trove of resources. A wonderful source for all sorts of international recipes and ingredients that might not be readily available where you live is ethnicgrocer.com. Also check out Epicurious.com and RecipeLand.com. If you are looking to rent foreign films that you can't find at your corner video store, check out 1worldfilms.com. And if you are looking for a great movie database to peruse, log onto imdb.com. Amazon.com not only has a huge selection of hard-to-find books, but also a vast catalog of international music, with free downloads so you can pick and choose just the kind of sound you want.

Above All, Enjoy

No matter where you decide to "go" or what you decide to do, make sure you are having fun. If you hate cooking, do take-out or splurge on going to a couple of restaurants from that country. The point is to break free from the routine of daily life and create a memorable, one-of-a-kind experience. We think you'll like it so much you'll choose to travel without leaving home over and over again!

—M. J. Ryan,
for the Editors of Conari Press

Brazen in Brazil

MMMM . . . Brazil! A place of mystery, music, and dance . . . where once a year (at least) the natives lose their minds and bodies in the revelry of *Carnaval!* A place where you can pair the extremes of nature living wild and free in the Amazon rainforest with the contrast of the cosmopolitan life in cities such as Rio de Janeiro and São Paulo. A place where Catholicism is the nationally recognized religion, yet Carnaval is one of the most notorious festivals in the world. Yes, Brazil is a true land of wonder, beauty, and paradox.

Setting the Scene

Brazil was "discovered" in 1500, when Pedro Alvares Cabral arrived there by accident on his way to India. In 1531, King Joao III of Portugal sent the first settlers to Brazil, and in 1534, divided the coast into twelve captaincies. The settlers found the soil to be fertile for growing sugar cane, and proceeded to put the Indians in the area to work as slave labor. During the seventeenth century, African slaves replaced the Indians on the plantations; this was not to last long, however. Runaway slaves developed bands known as Quilomilios who hid until 1888, when slavery was abolished. So the mix of cultures among Africa, Portugal, Europe, and indigenous peoples makes for a beautiful, diverse race.

Brazil is the world's fifth largest country, stretching across almost half of South America, and includes the richly forested

Amazon basin. The Amazon contains both the world's largest river (at 3,890 miles) and one of the world's largest forests. The Amazon forest alone contains 30 percent of the world's remaining forests, and largely accounts for the incredible numbers of wildlife thriving in the region. Brazil ranks number one in the categories of species of primates, amphibians, and plants, with insects and arachnids not far behind. Jaguars, spider monkeys, sloths, armadillos, boa constrictors, and anacondas are only a few of the varied species that exist there. Approximately 15,000 species call the Amazon home; this doesn't begin to account for the thousands of fish, birds, and insect life that have yet to be classified! Of course, the threat of extinction is imminent, due to the depletion of the rainforest.

Brazil tends to be hot most of the year. This means, of course, while planning your armchair travel, you should stick with light summer clothing—Brazilians love colorful clothing, with white saved for festivals and parades.

If you're really going to do Brazil as an armchair traveler, your best bet would be to plan a party. Turn up the music, cook lots of food, invite all your friends, and plan to stay up till all hours. And what better Brazilian party to plan than that in honor of one of the most well-known festivals in the world—Carnaval!

Carnaval literally means "farewell to the flesh" in Latin. It begins the Friday before Lent, at midnight. Lent is the forty-day period of prayers and reflection before Easter, in which Catholics are required to give up flesh; in other words, no meat. So who can blame anyone for wanting one big final hur-rah? This festival goes on for a period of five days, culminating in a huge celebration on Shrove Tuesday. (Shrove Tuesday, incidentally, has become famous in America and other parts of the world by a more famous name: Fat Tuesday, or Mardi Gras. Today, this tradition has spread to Venezuela, Colombia, Trinidad, Tobago, Mexico, Spain, and some parts of Italy. These countries have incorporated their own traditions into the religious theme of Carnaval and have made it their own.)

Carnaval celebrations are held all over Brazil; however, the one in Rio de Janeiro is known to be the most spectacular. Seven million Cariocas (as Rio's residents are called) swarm out to the streets to enjoy the Sambadromo, a tiered street designed expressly for the samba parades. In the Sambadromo, the top samba schools around Brazil get a chance to show their stuff: each band performs for about an hour, while the people dance in the streets. So be sure to include dancing in your lineup of activities, if only in dance videos.

To set the stage for your own Carnaval, think color, color, *color!* Streamers, beads, feathers, flowers, all in bright, bright colors! Brazilians love color in their festivals, so have as much on hand as you can. Drape colored beads and streamers around doorways. Be sure to have lots of candles available to set the mood. Remember, Carnaval is at its heart a religious celebration, so candles and incense are completely appropriate. To keep the cost down, votive candles are a wonderful option for a party; they burn for two to three hours, leave little mess to clean up, and are inexpensive, too! Most of these items you can find at a dollar store or drugstore in your area.

As a group activity, face and body painting is always fun. Since you shouldn't be wearing much anyway (Brazil is hot, remember), you'll have plenty of skin available for your friends to work on! Non-toxic paint can usually be purchased at a local art store or even a drugstore. While face painting might be fun, masks play an integral part of Carnaval; so why not try making your own? All you need are scissors, construction paper, string (to tie the mask on), and you're set! You can have fun making your own faces, and cutting whatever shapes you'd like your masks to be. At Carnaval, while the people might not wear

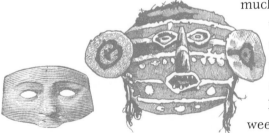

much, traditionally masks are usually worn to "fool the wandering evil spirits." They're also worn as protection, in case you end up doing something you shouldn't! Remember, as you plan your weekend, Brazilians are known to be a warm-hearted people, always ready to enjoy a festival, a parade, or simply a moment. Imagine away, and enjoy yours!

Books

If you are an art lover, be sure to take a look at *Latin American Art,* edited by Edward J. Sullivan. It features Brazilian artists such as Victor Brecheret, Candido Portirari, and the noteworthy Anita Mafatti, who inspired the modern art movement in Brazil with her own interpretation of Cubism. It's quite interesting to see Cubism from a woman's point of view, instead of the ubiquitous (albeit wonderful) examples of Picasso's Cubist art.

If you're more interested in reading about the history of Brazil, *The Brazilians,* by Joseph A. Page, is an excellent read. It tells the story of the true Brazil, once filled with as much violence as beauty. Page begins at the "discovery" of Brazil by Cabral and continues to its ongoing struggles with the modern-day economy.

If a history lesson is not what you're seeking, try *Traveler's Tales: Brazil,* edited by Haddock & Dogett, in which true stories are told about life on the road, or in the jungle, as it were. A particular favorite of mine is a story called "Alone and Unarmed," by Petru Popescue, a writer who was abandoned by the Mayoreina tribe in the Amazon rainforest. He describes the beauty he sees, in contrast to the fear he feels as he is witness to a struggle for survival. He runs across a baby jaguar who feeds for the first time on live prey. It's quite a counterpoint, as the beauty and the violence in his piece seem irrevocably interwoven. These short stories are ideal to read aloud, since none is longer than eight to ten pages.

In that same vein, Peter Fleming's *Brazilian Adventure* tells the story of the search for renowned English adventurer Colonel P. H. Fowlett, who disappeared in the jungles of Brazil in 1932. This story is done autobiographically, from Fleming's point of view. Fleming, a well-known editor, takes a year off to travel 3,000 miles with his compatriots through the Amazon jungle, searching for clues to this mystery. Although it was originally written in 1933, it remains a timeless adventure classic.

Samba, by Alma Guillermoprieto, is a firsthand account of life in the *favelas* (ghettoes) that surround Rio de Janiero. Ms. Guillermoprieto, a dancer and journalist, decided to spend a year in one of these favelas, called Magueira. She tells a fascinating story and relates in full detail the paradox between the poorest citizens of Rio, who are primarily black and who live for this time of year, for the dance; and their white counterparts, who watch and participate for entertainment only. An absorbing and sensual read, *Samba* gives you a true sense of how important music, song, and dance are to the indigenous people of Brazil.

Trying to get your children excited about Carnaval? I'd suggest *Carnaval,* written by George Ancona. Beautifully photographed, this wonderful children's book captures the essence of Carnaval in the small town of Olinda, Brazil. With vivid pictures of both adults and children, this book takes you through the preparation the town makes for Carnaval, the actual five days, and the peace that follows on Ash Wednesday, with easily read text. Although this is a children's book, it appealed to me as a "Carnaval for Beginners," because of its simple and straightforward descriptions and explanations. What a great way to get your child excited and involved in your "armchair travels"!

*M*ovies

Brazil is such a beautiful place that your imagination can run amok, just as it has for so many directors who have found it a beautiful, natural place to shoot films. Depending on your mood, one of these three films should suit!

Central Station, directed by Walter Salles, was touted as one of the best films, foreign or otherwise, of 1998. Set in Rio de Janeiro, a young boy (played wonderfully by Vinicus de Oliveira) loses his mother in a tragic accident out in front of the Central Station in Rio. He encounters a retired schoolteacher who reluctantly takes an interest in him. The movie takes them on a journey from Rio to the outermost region in Northwest Brazil on a search for the boy's father. A heart-wrenching, beautiful story in every sense of the word, *Central Station* is a fine film that will appeal to almost anyone.

Tearjerkers not to your taste? *4 Days in September* (1997), directed by Bruno Barreto, might interest you. A thriller set in Brazil, this suspenseful film is based on fact. An American ambassador (Alan Arkin) is kidnapped by terrorists and held for four days, while an uncomfortable American consulate decides what his fate should be. Filled with both intrigue and suspense, this Academy Award-nominated film successfully conveys the emotion and frustration Arkin's character feels, caught between the fear of the terrorists and the horror of not being valuable enough to be saved by his own people.

Barreto takes a completely different tack in his newest film, *Bossa Nova* (2000). This light romantic comedy shows the beauty of Brazil through the eyes of a man, his wife, and a widowed American schoolteacher, played quite wonderfully by Amy Irving, who are involved in a romantic triangle. This film is filled with truly skillful performances, as well as with quirky characters seemingly pulled out from nowhere.

All three of these films are in Portuguese, with English subtitles, but don't let that bother you. Subtitles have improved in the past ten years; these movies are quite easily understood.

Music

The Samba Step Amalgamation

The *samba* is truly a Brazilian original. Developed from a mixture of Spanish *bolero* and African rhythms, the music (as well as the dance) became popular during the 1930s and has never lost its appeal. The dance originated in Bahia, the northeast province of Brazil, and focuses on both ancient cadences and the rhythmic belly movements of African dance.

Dance and music are impossibly intertwined in Brazilian culture: music is called the dance, and vice versa. Other dances and music sprung from Brazilian soil are the *lambada* (music influenced by the Caribbean) and the *bossa nova*. The lambada is still popular today, both as a dance and a form of music, while the bossa nova (inspired by North American jazz) was popular in Brazil during the 1950s and '60s. Nevertheless, the *samba* will always be considered the national dance music of Brazil!

While you must have music for your Carnaval party, the choice of music can be a bit confusing. I suggest *Brasil: A Century of Song* as a beginner's course in Brazilian music. This four-volume CD collection covers four time periods: Folk and Traditional Music, Carnaval, the Bossa Nova Era, and MPB, or *Musica Popular Brasiliera.* Each CD is approximately an hour long, and the set contains a 48-page full-color book describing the history of music in Brazil. My personal favorite was on the Carnaval CD, a song called "Bathques de Samba." While I couldn't keep up, it was fun trying! I suggest volumes 2 and 4 for your party; they are more Carnaval-like and are conducive to a dance atmosphere.

Doing the Samba

Step back with your right foot, step forward a half-step with your left, and bring your right foot back to its original position. Repeat, starting with your left foot; step back, step forward a half-step with your right, bring your left back to original position. It's that easy!

Of course, the trick is to do this step as fast as you can to the music, while shaking your hips and buttocks as hard as you can. Samba music is energetic, lively, and fast. You knew there had to be a catch, didn't you?

Food

Brazilians tend to eat late in the evening; normal dining hours can be anywhere from 7 to 11 P.M. So prepare for a party that might last till the wee hours of the morning! That is, if you truly do this Brazilian style.

What follows here is one complete dinner. If you'd like more ideas for recipes, try *Delightful Brazilian Cooking* by Eng Tie Ang. This is an extremely easy how-to cookbook with approximately 130 recipes to sink your teeth into. Or, if you're feeling more adventurous, try Steven Raichler's *Healthy Latin Cooking Cookbook.* This book incorporates Cuban and Caribbean as well as Brazilian recipes. There's a wonderful introduction that gives you a bit of history on every region that is addressed in the book, and the full-color pictures are beautiful. *Eat Smart in Brazil* by Joan and David Peterson is an easy, no-nonsense approach to Brazilian cooking. Here the authors incorporate funny little cultural anecdotes in with the recipes, as well as marvelous photographs. Finally, consider *The Art of Brazilian Cookery* by Dolores Botafogo. It was written in 1960, but is still a staple in many Brazilian kitchens today. This is a very straightforward cookbook that incorporates the use of Brazilian terms, such as the word *refogado,* which is untranslatable in English; the closest definition would be a sauté of tomatoes, onion, and garlic. This wonderful cookbook truly gives you a sense of the *flavor* of Brazil.

Caipirinha

To have Carnaval, you must start off with a pitcher of Caipirinhas, the favored drink among Brazilians. You can use oranges, lemons, or grapefruits to make this wonderful punch. But be careful, it's quite strong!

4 limes, halved

10 tablespoons sugar

Ice cubes

$^3/_4$ cup *cachaca* (if you cannot find it, use vodka or light rum)

Squeeze lime juice into a bowl. Remove seeds; do not remove pulp. Add sugar and cachaca. Fill glasses with ice cubes; pour over ice. Serves 4.

Forbidden Fruit

Brazil is well known for its fruit, many of which are only available in the region where they grow. Guarana, steeped in tradition and folklore, is one of the best-loved fruits of Brazil. It is said that the fruit has a resemblance to the human eye when ripe; this has sparked a legend among the Satare-Maue Indians of a beautiful woman named Onhiamuacabe, who gave birth to a child sired by an unknown entity. This child was put to death, apparently, for eating forbidden fruit (or nuts—the legend has several versions) and at his burial site, a Guarana bush began to grow. Some believe that this bush is responsible for bringing forth the beginnings of the Maue tribe of Brazil. To the Indians, the seeds of this fruit had power both as a stimulant and an aphrodisiac. We know now that this stimulant is actually caffeine, which of course many Americans have a fondness for!

Moqueca de Camarao

Although the Brazilian diet is made up primarily of white rice, black beans, and manioc—a staple you'll find at almost every Brazilian table, similar to a coarse meal or flour that's rich in carbohydrates—it includes spicy dishes as well. Now that you've warmed your guests' palates, prepare them for one of Brazil's specialties, Moqueca de Camaro, a seafood stew flavored with coconut milk. This will remind you of New Orleans; remember, Brazil's largest single influence in cuisine came from African slaves, as did much of New Orleans cooking. This dish is best served over rice.

1 onion, finely chopped	2 tablespoons vegetable oil
1 clove garlic, minced	3 tablespoons tomato paste
2 tablespoons vinegar	1 teaspoon black pepper, or to taste
Juice of 1 lemon	1 cup whole milk
1 teaspoon salt	½ lb. crab meat, picked over
1 lb. fresh shrimp, shelled and deveined	1 cup coconut milk

Combine the onion, garlic, vinegar, lemon juice, and salt, and marinate the shrimp in this mixture for an hour prior to cooking. Pour the oil into pan with tomato paste and pepper, stirring frequently to keep from sticking. When hot, add shrimp and whole milk; cook over low heat until shrimp are cooked. Add crab meat; let simmer for approximately 10 minutes. Add coconut milk; cook for another 5 minutes. Serves 4.

Couvé Minera

(COOKED KALE)

While African American recipes often incorporate kale (and other greens) into their cooking, Brazilians tend to sauté rather than boil their vegetables. A bit of a different taste, but just as good!

1 lb. kale	2 tablespoons tomato paste
1 clove garlic, minced	4 tablespoons olive oil
½ onion, minced	

Wash and drain kale thoroughly (this might take several washings). Sauté garlic, onion, and tomato paste in oil, making sure paste does not stick. Add kale; cook over medium heat for 3–5 minutes.

Mungunza

(HOMINY DESSERT)

2 15-oz. cans white hominy	1 cup unsalted peanuts, roasted and
2 cups whole milk	ground
6 oz. sweetened condensed milk	1 teaspoon nutmeg
1 cup coconut milk	

Drain hominy and place in a medium saucepan. Add milk and cook over low heat for 15 minutes or until hominy is soft, stirring occasionally. Add condensed milk, coconut milk, and peanuts. Simmer for another 15 minutes, stirring occasionally. Chill for 4 hours. When serving, sprinkle nutmeg on top. Serves 8.

—Mignon Freeman

A Fling down Mexico Way

Setting the Scene

HOLA! Welcome to your very own *casa* away from *casa*. First and foremost, Mexico is a colorful and lively place, so turning your house into a hacienda should be fun. Mexican colors are red, white, yellow, and green; keep them in mind as you go about your decorating. To get yourself in the mood, try wearing clothing in these colors. String Christmas lights in the living or dining room. Or even better, get your hands on some strings of chili pepper-shaped lights! Paper streamers can be fun; they are inexpensive and can be found in any party store. And don't forget a colorful tablecloth.

No Mexican *fiesta* is complete without a piñata. Not just for kids, piñatas can add to everyone's weekend. They are available at Mexican markets or party stores, but you can easily construct your own. Get a very large balloon and blow it up. Cut up newspaper in ½-inch strips. Dip each strip into a bowl of undiluted laundry starch. Then wrap the strip around the balloon. Continue until the balloon is completely covered. Allow to dry, then paint with poster paint and cut a hole in the top (the balloon will pop; that's okay) to drop the treats in. Fill the balloon with candy, small gifts, nuts. On either side of the big hole, cut a small hole and insert a strong cord for the hanger. Suspend with a rope and pulley so it can be raised and lowered when you and your guests take turns whacking it with a stick while blindfolded. When it breaks, go wild for the goodies!

Books

For an incredible visual feast, try browsing through *Henri Cartier-Bresson: Mexican Notebooks* by Henri Cartier-Bresson and Carlos Fuentes, a remarkable photographic look at everyday life in Mexico between 1934 and 1964.

A terrific travel essay on Mexico, exploring the human spirit as felt in Mexico, is Tony Cohan's *On*

Mexican Time. It's the story of how he and his wife found a new life in a sixteenth-century hill town in Mexico. He is poetic in his description of sights, scents, sounds, colors, and aromas.

If you're interested in Mexican art, check out the work of Diego Rivera and Frida Kahlo. Pete Hamill's book *Diego Rivera* has 107 illustrations. Or try reading some of *The Diary of Frida Kahlo: An Intimate Self-portrait.* But be forewarned: It will put your Spanish skills to work!

Like Water for Chocolate by Laura Esquivel is a perfect book for a weekend stay-at-home. It can be read in short installments, and it even has great recipes throughout it! It's sexy, romantic, and brings you right into the heart of Mexican culture.

Carlos Fuentes, one of the greatest Mexican novelists of all time, offers plenty of books to choose from. *The Old Gringo* imagines the fate of Ambrose Bierce, the celebrated American writer and soldier who disappeared in Mexico. Fuentes' recent novel, *The Years with Laura Díaz,* follows the life of one woman from the Revolution of 1910 to the Tlatelolco Massacre of 1968. It sweeps across twentieth-century Mexico exploring politics, history, and culture within a fascinating story filled with love, tragedy, and the human spirit.

Or you might want to read the works of American authors who write about Mexico. John Steinbeck's *Log from the Sea of Cortez* details the author's travels on a sardine boat out of Monterey,

California, on a 4,000-mile voyage around the Baja Peninsula in the Sea of Cortez; Malcolm Lowry's *Under the Volcano* has also been called a great piece of literature about Mexico.

Just for fun, an interesting and amusing book is *Mexican Sayings: The Treasure of a People* by Octavio Ballesteros. In it you will uncover *dichos* such as "My house is your house," and "Old is the sun and it still shines."

Videos

For your video entertainment, remember that *The Old Gringo* (1989) and *Like Water for Chocolate* (1992) were both made into great films; they capture the same elements that the books do.

El Mariachi (1993) and *Desperado* (1995) are two great films by Robert Rodríguez that are action packed and convey a sense of Mexico. *El Mariachi* won an award at the Sundance Film Festival, and although low budget, it is a high-energy, graphically violent, creative film about a mariachi player who is mistaken for a killer. *Desperado* picks up where *El Mariachi* leaves off.

The Mask of Zorro (1998) takes place in the early nineteenth century, when the elder Zorro comes out of retirement to train a new Zorro to fight the enemy Montero.

If you are looking for more of a travelogue, consider *Barroco* (1990), a narrativeless film that is a series of images, music, and sounds that transports you through Mexico's history.

Music

As for Mexican music, there is a wide variety ranging from mariachi to pop-rock. Compilations are always a good route to take because they give samples of many different bands. The Rough Guide, the company that puts out travel books, also puts out a CD compilation called *Tex-Mex,* which features a variety of music from the Tex-Mex border that might be perfect for your weekend.

Here are some other good musical selections: *100 Años de Mariachi* by various artists is a CD filled with passionate mariachi music. *The Mexican Revolution* boxed set is inexpensive and features music from as early as 1904 through the 1970s. *Mexico's Greatest Hits* by Los Capacaba is so authentic, you'll think you're on vacation in Mexico.

Maná is a pop Mexican band that is very popular; check out their 1994 album *En Vivo.* Selena's *Dreaming of You* became even more popular after her tragic death.

Did You Know . . .

- There is a festival every day of the year in one city or another in Mexico, including the Night of the Radishes on December 23 in Oaxaca commemorating the introduction of the radish by Spanish colonists. Artists carve radishes for a competition!

- Mariachi bands use a variety of instruments including violins, guitars, basses, and trumpets. They sing of love and betrayal, death and politics.

- Hot chocolate originated in Mexico as a drink for royalty.

- Alaska was at one time part of Mexico.

- The first people known to have used the peanut were the Mayas of Mexico.

- Peanuts, vanilla, guavas, tomatoes, some forty different chilies, avocados, and papaya all came from Mexico.

- Chewing gum originated in Mexico from the Zapote Blanco tree. William Wrigley, along with Thomas Adams and John Colgan, noticed that its resin hardened when exposed to air.

First you need the basics. Begin by cutting wedges of lime and arranging them on a plate. The soft acidity of the lime complements any Mexican dish. And don't forget chips and salsa (see recipe)! Another specialty on the Mexican table is chili salt, which should be served in a tiny pot and sprinkled over food.

Food

The popularity of Mexican food in the United States is a testament to the tastiness of a great variety of dishes from this country. It is often said that "cuisine is culture"; the food of Mexico attests to its own history. For example, the diet in pre-Columbian times was based predominantly on corn, which was native to the land. After the Conquest, the country's cuisine changed dramatically with Spanish influence; rice, olives, wine, and spices are now common. Imagination and improvisation are key, so feel free to experiment with the recipes. Here are some of the basics to make one dinner. To find other great recipes, try *Recipe of Memory: Five Generations of Mexican Cuisine* by Víctor and Mary Lau Valle. *The Art of Mexican Cooking* by Diane Kennedy is another popular one, and Patricia Quintana's *The Taste of Mexico* is so beautifully photographed, you'll want to try every recipe!

When planning your menu, don't forget the tequila. Tequila, particularly served as shots with salt and lime wedges, is *the* drink of Mexico. It is often referred to as "the respectable Mexican beverage." It has existed since the early 1700s, when Spaniards began distilling the Indian beverage *pulque,* made from the agave plant. However, tequila is not just a drink for shots and margaritas; it can be sipped and savored like a fine brandy or scotch. Tequila is named for a place—a town in the state of Jalisco, thirty-five miles northwest of Guadalajara.

Keep in mind that there are different qualities of tequila. By law, tequila must be at least 51 percent agave in order to be called "tequila"; the cheaper varieties can be filled with sugars, coloring, and flavoring and only matured for a few weeks. Tequilas labeled 100 percent agave should not contain any other fermentable sugars. One of the best brands of tequila is Herradura Seleccion Suprema. At $225–$250 a bottle, it is truly supreme. The only other tequila that comes close to this one is Cuervo Reserva de la Familia. For something a bit less pricey, try Jose Cuervo 1800 *añejo* (not to be confused with Cuervo 1800!), made of 100 percent blue agave añejo. Like the Reserva de la Familia, it has a full oak flavor and smooth finish. Herradura añejo is a consistently good tequila with a fruity aroma and little aftertaste. Alteno is a good tequila for the price and has a strong agave flavor.

Toasting Etiquette

In Mexican tradition, while drinking tequila, with the first shot you give a toast to *salud* (health). The second is a toast to *amor* (love), the third *dinero* (money), and the fourth *tiempo para disfrutarlos* (time to enjoy them).

Salsa

The usual ingredients of Mexican salsas are red tomato, onion, garlic, chilies, and cilantro. Many other ingredients may be used, such as seeds, nuts, fruits, and in the case of mole, chocolate. Make your salsas hotter or milder by adjusting the number of chilies used.

1 medium onion, chopped	4 small green chilies, seeded and diced
3 ripe tomatoes, chopped	2 teaspoons salt
½ cup fresh chopped cilantro	2 teaspoons lime juice

Mix all ingredients in serving bowl. Taste and adjust seasonings if needed. Serves 6.

Bring On the Beer

If you are looking for alcoholic beverages for your weekend, be sure to stock up on Mexican beer *(cerveza)* as well: Corona, Sol, or Tecate. These are great beach beers especially in the hot summertime. They are light and refreshing. That's because Mexico, for the most part, produces lager beers, using a type of yeast that ferments at a lower temperature; the result is a smoother, lighter, and less biting beer. Corona, Chihuahua, Pacífico, and Sol are some of the superlight Mexican beers. Although Corona is the most popular in the United States, the others have more of a distinctive flavor.

The most popular Mexican beer in Mexico tends to be a light to medium lager such as Dos Equis Special Lager XX, Tecate, and Carta Blanca. Dos Equis Special Lager is a great pick. Dos Equis was established just before 1900, and the XX refers to the approaching twentieth century. Tecate is brewed in the northern Mexican town of, you guessed it, Tecate!

While harder to find, Mexico does produce some full-bodied beers, including Negra Modelo and Dos Equis Amber. Negra Modelo is both sweet and bitter, and deliciously creamy in the mouth. Dos Equis Amber is also rich and smooth.

Guacamole

Guacamole starts to go brown within about an hour, so make this just before you want to use it. Putting an avocado pit into the guacamole helps to slow the discoloration.

3 ripe avocados

2 cloves garlic, crushed

1 small green chili, seeded and diced

1½ tablespoons lemon juice

½ teaspoon salt

1 tablespoon chopped cilantro
   (optional)

In a medium bowl, mash avocados with a fork, add remaining ingredients, and serve immediately

Chili Salt

This can substitute for the salt called for in any of the recipes included here and can be served on the table as a condiment. It keeps for weeks in an airtight container.

¼ cup chili powder

⅛ teaspoon ground cloves

1 teaspoon cayenne

¼ cup salt

Combine ingredients thoroughly. Makes ½ cup.

Mexican Gazpacho

This Spanish soup made the journey to Mexico, where it has taken on a life of its own—the Mexican version is usually more zesty than its Spanish cousin. Like most other tomato dishes, it tastes better the second day, so if you can make it a day in advance, that's great. To peel the tomatoes, drop them in boiling water for 20 seconds, remove, and, when cool enough to handle, peel them.

3 pounds ripe tomatoes

2 cups water

½ cup fresh lemon juice

1 medium cucumber, peeled, seeded, and chopped

1 jalapeño, seeded and chopped

½ medium onion, diced

1 large garlic clove, pressed

Salt to taste

1 tablespoon chopped fresh oregano

1 medium avocado, peeled and chopped

Strips of tortilla chips

Peel the tomatoes and purée in a blender or food processor. In a large bowl, stir together the tomatoes, water, lemon juice, cucumber, pepper, onion, garlic, salt, and oregano. Cover and refrigerate until very cold. Pour into bowls. Top with avocado chunks and tortilla chips. Serves 6.

Chicken Fajitas

Fajitas are very popular these days. This is a very simple and delicious version that is relatively low fat as well. Top with homemade salsa and guacamole!

2 cloves garlic, crushed

1 teaspoon dried oregano

½ teaspoon cumin powder

2 tablespoons orange juice

2 tablespoons white vinegar

1 dash Tabasco

1 lb. chicken breasts, skin trimmed off and
cut into thin strips

1 medium onion, peeled and thinly sliced

1 medium red pepper, seeded and thinly sliced

8 flour tortillas

Salsa and guacamole

Combine the first six ingredients in a shallow glass dish. Add the chicken and turn to thoroughly coat. Allow to marinate at least 15 minutes or up to 1 hour.

Remove meat from marinade and pour marinade into a large frying pan. Heat on high and add the onions and peppers. Cook in marinade for 5 minutes, or until beginning to wilt. Add the chicken, and stir fry until the juices run clear. Warm the tortillas, and serve with salsa and guacamole. Serves 4.

Mexican Rice

Mexican rice should be fluffy, not sticky. Here's a method to ensure that it turns out right.

1½ cups white rice

3 tablespoons oil

½ medium onion, chopped

2 garlic cloves, minced

3 cups chicken stock

Salt to taste

Wash the rice, then place in a container and cover with hot tap water. Soak for 20 minutes. Drain the rice, then rinse under cold running water until water runs clear.

Heat oil in a saucepan and add rice, onion, and garlic. Sauté until rice begins to change color (8–10 minutes). Add chicken stock and salt to taste. Bring to a boil and cook uncovered until most of the liquid has been absorbed. Cover and turn heat to lowest setting for 5 minutes. Remove from heat and let sit, covered, for 30 minutes. Fluff and serve. Serves 3–4.

Marvelous Margaritas

2 lime wedges	4 oz. tequila
Coarse salt, on a plate	1 oz. Grand Marnier
Ice	3 oz. fresh lime juice

Rub the rim of 2 glasses with the limes and dip glass rims into the salt. Fill a cocktail shaker with ice and add remaining ingredients. Shake well. Pour into the prepared glasses and garnish with the lime wedges. Serves 2.

Berry Ice

Fruit vendors of all sorts can be found throughout Mexico. They sell everything from fresh fruit to fruit purée in a wax paper cone. Fruit ice makes a delicious dessert or simply a nice refreshing drink. If you want more of a kick, you can add tequila. Tequila prevents this from freezing solid, which makes it easier to scoop out.

6 cups berries of your choosing, washed and stems removed	$1/3$ cup sugar
	3 tablespoons tequila (optional)

Place the berries and sugar in a blender or food processor and process until smooth. Pour into large bowl. Stir in the tequila if using. Cover and place bowl in the freezer for about

2 hours, until frozen around edges and top. Remove from freezer and whisk or beat with an electric beater so the mixture is evenly slushy. Cover and place back in the freezer until completely frozen (about 2–3 hours). Allow to soften at room temperature for 1 hour before serving. Serves 4.

Mexican Hot Chocolate

This is a traditional drink good for a wintry weekend.

4 cups milk (can be low- or nonfat)

3 cinnamon sticks broken in half

30 whole cloves

5 oz. semisweet chocolate, chopped

2 tablespoons unsweetened cocoa powder

2 tablespoons brown sugar

Bring milk, cinnamon, and cloves to a simmer in saucepan. Add remaining ingredients and mix until chocolate is melted. Remove from heat and allow to sit, covered, for 45 minutes. Serves 4.

—Julie Kessler

Kick Up Your Heels in Scotland

AH, SCOTLAND— land of green isles, mythical lakes, men in kilts, and Madonna's latest wedding. The beauty and character of Scotland's culture provide many options for the armchair traveler. To set the scene for a Scotland adventure at home, bring out the tartans, grab some tin whistles and wool sweaters, and don't forget the pint glasses. (Tartans are the traditional brightly colored plaid cloths that were worn as markers of the clan ties in medieval times. Today, kilts are worn by men, always above the knee and with nothing underneath.)

Setting the Scene

If there is soccer on the television, turn it up, root for your favorite team passionately, and remember that in Scotland, soccer is called *football*. If you have a feel for the accent, be sure to give it a try when chatting with your friends and loved ones. Rolling your *r*'s is one of the first steps, but it is definitely an acquired talent. If a sip of whisky blows you away, then say you feel "dead brilliant." And after a long day of Scotland at home you may feel "dead tired."

If you happen to have any coats of arms in the attic, bring them down and hang them on the walls. Posters of rolling green hills and a gorgeous landscape will add to the scene. And as a final touch, consider hiring a bagpiper to get the weekend rolling. With fabulous food and splendid song, you will have an enchanting time in Scotland from your very own home!

Books

Here are two coffee-table books perfect for browsing. Full of breathtaking scenery and colorful history, *Heritage of Scotland: A Cultural History of Scotland and Its People* by Nathaniel Harris is a lavishly illustrated book that examines major events and figures in Scottish history, as well as the culture and traditions of the Scottish people. *Portrait of Scotland* by Colin Baxter features enchanting photographs of the best of Scotland, from Glasgow and Edinburgh to the Isle of Skye, the Orkneys, and Inverness, by Scotland's most famous photographer.

The greatest Scottish poet ever, Robert Burns, has written many anthems of Scottish life. From "Auld Lang Syne" to "Address to a Haggis," Burns' poems would be a great addition to any Scottish weekend. Pick up a copy of *Robert Burns: Selected Poems,* and stand in the corner and read aloud to your bonnie lass or lad.

If poetry is not your thing, consider reading prose out loud. *Scottish Fairy Tales* by Dover Publishing offers a collection of eight Scottish fairy tales for kids and adults alike, from "Battle of the Fairy Kings" to "Conall and the Thunder Hag."

If you are inclined to spend a weekend or more sitting by the fire reading a novel, consider the books of Scottish author Dorothy Dunnett, who has been hailed as the greatest living writer of historical fiction in the world. She's also prolific; there are six novels in the Lymond Chronicles (full of the swashbuckling antics of a sixteenth-century Scottish James Bond who recites classical poetry while saving Mary, Queen of Scots) and eight in the House of Niccolo. But beware: Her work is habit forming.

Sing a Song

Here is the classic song, written by Robert Burns, in both traditional Scottish and modern-day English. Try singing both and see which you prefer!

Traditional Scottish Version . . .

Auld Lang Syne

Should auld acquaintance be forgot,
And never brought to mind?
Should auld acquaintance be forgot,
And auld lang syne?

Chorus:

For auld lang syne, my jo,
For auld lang syne,
We'll tak a cup o' kindness yet

For auld lang syne.
And surely you'll be your pint-stowp,
And surely I'll be mine,
And we'll tak a cup o' kindness yet
For auld lang syne!

Chorus

We twa hae ran about the braes,
And pu'd the gowans fine,
But we've wander'd monie a weary fit
Sin' auld lang syne.

Chorus

Modern English Translation . . .

Days Long Ago

Should old acquaintances be forgotten
And never be remembered?
Should old acquaintances be forgotten
and days long ago.

Chorus:

For days long ago, my dear,
For days long ago
We'll drink a cup of kindness yet
For days long ago!

And surely you'll have your pint tankard
And surely I'll have mine.
And we'll drink a cup of kindness yet
For days long ago.

Chorus

We two have run about the hills
And pulled the daisies fine
But we've wandered many a weary mile
Since the days long ago.

Chorus

We twa hae paidl'd in the burn	We two have paddled in the stream
Frae morning sun til dine,	From morning sun till dinnertime
But seas between us braid hae roar'd	But the broad seas have roared between us
Sin' auld lang syne.	Since the days long ago.
Chorus	Chorus
And there's a hand, my trusty fiere,	And here's my hand, my trusty friend,
And gie's a hand o' thine,	And give me your hand too,
And we'll tak a right guid-willie waught	And we will take an excellent good-will drink
For auld lang syne!	For the days of long ago.
Chorus	Chorus

Meaning of unusual words:

auld lang syne = former days and friends
gowans = daisies
jo = dear
braid = broad
stowp = tankard
guid-willie waught = friendly draught

Robert Burns

Videos

CARRICKFERGUS CASTLE

Braveheart (1995). Set in thirteenth-century Scotland, this sweeping epic starring and directed by Mel Gibson is the partly historical, partly mythological story of William Wallace, a Scottish common man who fights for his country's freedom from English rule. Chock-full of honor and battle scenes, this movie provides more than a glimpse of the incredible nationalism of the Scottish.

Rob Roy (1995). In the highlands of Scotland in the 1700s, Rob Roy, played by Liam Neeson, fights to lead his small town to a better future. He becomes a Robin Hood-style renegade and must defend his family and honor.

Breaking the Waves (1996). This tragic drama is set in a deeply religious community in the north of Scotland, where a naïve young woman goes to great lengths for love. The plot line may be tough for some to watch, but the scenery is incredible, with storming coastal views and rolling hills.

Trainspotting (1996). Set in contemporary times, this movie takes you on a trip through the unrelenting darkest parts of Edinburgh heroin addicts and disaffected Scottish youth. Not for the faint of heart, this film is an exhilarating and disturbing portrait of lives on the edge.

Music

There are wonderful traditional and contemporary CDs that provide a sampling of the great music that has come out of Scotland. Here are a few to consider:

The Fiddler's Dance by the Scottish Fiddle Orchestra is a collection of fine and enjoyable Scottish fiddle dance music that will bring you all the fun of a traditional Scottish dance party. From waltzes to polkas, this recording will inspire you to dance all around the house.

The Best Ever Scottish Compilation. All the best of Scottish music, both traditional and contemporary. If you are looking for one CD to play over and over, this is it. This collection offers music to dance to as well as more relaxing fare from legendary musicians such as Jimmy Shand MBE to modern bands like the Porridge Men and Enter the Haggis.

The Man Who by Travis. Travis is a Scottish quartet that captures the essence of their homeland, with longing melodies and haunting poetic lyrics on this great "Brit-rock" CD.

If You're Feeling Sinister by Belle and Sebastian. This is gentle and dreamy folk pop from a seven-piece pop orchestra from Glasgow, Scotland. Great music to listen to from the top of a mountain overlooking the ocean or from the warmth of your bed.

Food

While the best-known Scottish food is probably haggis, a delicacy made from sheep's organs boiled inside a sheep's stomach, this may be a bit labor intensive for a relaxing weekend. If you are inclined to prepare it, a quick Internet search will turn up many recipes, including a nontraditional vegetarian version.

If you have kids around, "fish and chips"—fried white fish, such as cod, and what Americans call "French fries" all wrapped together in newspaper and doused with vinegar and salt—would be appropriate Scottish fare. Contemporary Scottish snacks sold in hole-in-the-wall restaurants called "chippies" include baked potatoes with toppings like cheese, tuna, and canned corn, and even deep-fried pizza!

Here are a few recipes for some traditional treats that will leave you time afterward for a few warming Whisky Toddies. To find other authentic recipes, look at *Savory Scottish Recipes* by Julie J. McDonald, which contains dozens of traditional recipes, from Scottish Farmhouse Eggs to Chicken Stovies. It also provides anecdotes and traditional lore to complement the recipes.

Shortbread

A popular treat to nibble on morning, noon, and night.

4 oz. butter, softened

¹/₄ cup granulated sugar plus additional as topping

³/₄ cup white flour

2 tablespoons cornstarch

Cream the butter and sugar together until smooth. Using a sieve, add the flour and the cornstarch into the bowl. Stir until completely combined. Flour a board or table, and place the dough in the middle. Using a rolling pin, roll out about a quarter-inch thick. Cut into rounds with a biscuit cutter and prick several times with a fork.

Preheat oven to 325°F. Using a spatula, lift the shortbread onto an oiled cookie sheet. Bake for 25 minutes or until brown and crispy. Sprinkle sugar on the top of the shortbread immediately after it has been removed from the oven. Allow to cool completely, and store in an airtight tin. Serves 4.

Shepherd's Pie

Sheep have been a main food supply for Scotland; thus lamb forms the basis for many traditional dishes.

1 lb. boneless lamb, minced

1 large onion, chopped

½ lb. mushrooms, chopped

2 carrots, diced

1 bay leaf

4 tablespoons white flour

1 cup beef or vegetable stock

1 tablespoon ketchup

water

1½ lbs. boiling potatoes, peeled and
   cut into quarters

4 tablespoons low-fat milk

2 oz. Cheddar cheese, grated

Over medium heat, fry the lamb with the onion, mushrooms, carrots, and bay leaf for 10 minutes or until lamb and vegetables are cooked through. Add the flour, and stir until the flour is brown. Add the stock and ketchup, stirring constantly. Stir over medium-high heat until the mixture thickens. Reduce heat, cover, and simmer for 20 minutes, adding water if necessary. Remove the bay leaf and place mixture in a large casserole dish.

While the lamb is cooking, boil the potatoes until cooked, about 20 minutes. Drain well, then mash with milk. Preheat the oven to 400°F. Spread the mashed potatoes on top of the meat and sprinkle with the cheese. Bake until heated through and the top is browned, about 15 minutes. Serves 4.

Rumbledethumps

Originating in Ireland, this dish is now mass-produced and served in Scottish supermarkets. Here's how to make it yourself.

2 oz. butter	1 lb. boiled cabbage, drained and chopped
1 lb. mashed potatoes	salt and black pepper to taste

Melt the butter in a large saucepan over low heat. Mix in the potatoes and cabbage and heat slowly. Season to taste with salt and pepper, and serve piping hot. Serves 4.

Dundee Cake

This is a fruity and rich cake that is often served at Christmas, but is delicious year-round!

1 cup flour	³/₄ cup each currants, raisins, and
1 teaspoon baking powder	seedless white raisins
³/₄ cup butter	grated rind and juice of 1 lemon
¹/₂ cup granulated sugar	2 tablespoons whisky or water
4 eggs	2 tablespoons boiled milk with
1 oz. blanched almonds	1 tablespoon sugar stirred in
1¹/₂ oz. mixed orange and lemon peel	

Preheat oven to 325°F. In a small bowl, sift the flour and baking powder together. Set aside.

In a large bowl, cream the butter and sugar until fluffy, then add the eggs one at a time. Stir in the nuts, fruits, and lemon rind and juice. Add the flour mixture and the whisky or water, and mix well.

Place mixture in an 8-inch greased and lined cake tin. Flatten the top with damp hands. Cover with foil and bake for 2 hours or until a tester poked in the middle comes out clean.

Ten minutes before cake is done, brush the top with the sweetened milk. Cool in the pan for 15 minutes before turning out on a wire tray. Serves 8.

Whisky Toddy

A necessity if you have the sniffles, but also great if you don't.

Boiling water

1 tablespoon lemon juice

1 cube sugar cut into four pieces

2 oz. well-matured Scotch Whisky, such as Glenfiddich or Balmoran

Fill a large tumbler halfway with hot water. When the glass has reached a comfortable temperature, pour it out and put the sugar in the glass. Pour in a half-cup of boiling water and stir. When the sugar is dissolved, add the whisky and lemon juice and stir. Serves 1.

—*Rosie Levy*

Here's to Whisky

There are three types of Scotch whisky: malt, grain, and blended. Malt whisky is produced only from 100 percent malted barley. Grain whisky is produced from a variety of cereals that may or may not include a proportion of malted barley. Blended whisky is a combination of malt and grain whisky, mixed together in the same bottle. A whisky, however produced, may only be legally described as Scotch if it has matured in an oak cask in Scotland for a minimum of three years. It must also have been bottled at a minimum strength of 40 percent alcohol by volume.

Michael Jackson's Complete Guide to Single Malt Scotch: The Connoisseur's Guide to the Single Malt Whiskies of Scotland is full to the brim with maps, photos, and an overview of factors affecting production, such as geography and flavor components. This is the perfect book to take to your local liquor store when you are trying to select your authentic beverages.

Putting on the Green and the Guinness in Ireland

THE EMERALD Isle, as Ireland is otherwise known, is a place of lush green hills and pastures that lend themselves to the nickname. The rugged coastline and magnificent cliffs that surround this island reflect the indomitable spirit of its people and their ability to withstand enormous political and economic hardships.

Setting the Scene

Beneath the surface lies a rich heritage of culture and tradition that will make your armchair Ireland experience a pleasure.

Some of the world's finest and most beautiful handmade goods come from Ireland. You may already have these in your home to wear or display. If not, you can always use or buy something that resembles the original to set the stage for your weekend.

Hand knits

Perhaps the most familiar hand-knit item out of Ireland is the Aran sweater, hailing from the isles of the same name on the western side of Ireland. These heavy sweaters are typically worn by fishermen who want to stay warm under harsh conditions. Built to last a lifetime, the sweaters are made of undyed wool knit into intricate ropelike patterns that once identified a person's family and where they were from. Other hand-woven items include capes, throws, and mohair garments.

Lead crystal

Irish lead crystal, a combination of minerals and glass, is world famous. The best known of all is the hand-cut Waterford crystal, which derives its name from County Waterford in the southeast. Irish lead crystal is typically cut to create mesmerizing patterns that reflect the light wonderfully.

BELLEEK CHINA

Usually seen with a basketweave design and often hand-painted with little shamrocks, the distinct Belleek china comes from the old town of Belleek, where a factory still uses the same process that was invented in 1857.

TWEEDS

Tweed, a coarse woolen fabric that is typically used to make jackets and caps, has long been a part of Irish fashion. The weaving of Donegal tweed, with its roots in County Donegal, is among the greatest of unbroken traditions.

LINEN

Linen, a woven natural fiber of the flax plant and the oldest fabric known to man, is one of the most expensive fabrics made today, and Irish linen is regarded as the finest linen in the world. Often white and fine in its feel, it is used to make exquisite tableclothes, napkins, placemats, apparel, and bed sheets. It is the ultimate summer fabric because its absorbency and coolness keep the heat and humidity at bay, leaving the wearer cool and fresh.

Kissing the Blarney Stone

The Irish have a knack for what they call *craic* (pronounced "crack") or gab. It's also a word used to describe socializing, which can include chatting, listening, learning, gossiping, having a good time, and entertainment in general. The Blarney Stone, a stone located at the top of a 90-foot tower at Blarney Castle in County Cork, is said to give the gift of gab when kissed. Pubs, which are still among the pillars of Irish social life, are where a lot of *craic* takes place. You might want to consider gathering a group of friends to create such a spirited environment as part of your weekend.

At some point in the weekend, you might want to venture out-side for a game of Irish road bowling. This ancient sport is still played today in Ireland, where they hold national championship games every year. The object of the game is to be the first one to throw a ball three miles down the road, using the fewest number of shots. In Ireland, it is played with a "bullet" of cast iron weighing approximately twenty-two ounces. (Originally, they were cannonballs, hence the name.) For all practical purposes, you could substitute a tennis ball or a baseball for the bullet. The trick is to find a relatively quiet stretch of road without too much traffic!

Books

The Irish probably have more sayings, proverbs, and songs—certainly drinking songs— than any other culture. There are several books of Irish songs (one of the best is *The Words of 101 Irish Songs and Ballads*) and sayings (try *Irish Proverbs*) that can be found at bookstores or music stores. Sprinkle your week-end with a few of them and enhance the authenticity of your experience.

Ireland is rich in literary history, with four Nobel Prize-win-ners in literature: William Butler Yeats, George Bernard Shaw,

Samuel Beckett, and Seamus Heaney. Some of Ireland's other great writers include James Joyce, Oscar Wilde, Edna O'Brien, Maeve Binchy, Roddy Doyle, William Trevor, Flann O'Brien, and Frank McCourt. For a slice of Irish culture, I suggest the following books:

Angela's Ashes by Frank McCourt. The Pulitzer Prize-winning memoir of the author's young life in Limerick in Depression-era Ireland.

The Collected Poems of W. B. Yeats, edited by Richard J. Finneran. A comprehensive collection of poems by Ireland's beloved poet.

The Dubliners by James Joyce. In these short stories, Joyce creates a portrait of the Irish and his native city, Dublin.

The Mammy by Brendan O'Carroll. Popular Irish comedian Brendan O'Carroll chronicles with raw humor and great affection the comic misadventures of a large and lively North Dublin family in the 1960s.

Mother Ireland by Edna O'Brien. O'Brien captures the soul of Ireland and its people in this 1976 memoir. Weaving her own personal history with the history of Ireland, she melds local customs and ancient lore with the fascinating people and events that shaped her young life.

Paddy Clarke Ha Ha Ha by Roddy Doyle. In this Booker Prize-winning novel, Roddy Doyle charts the triumphs, indignities, and bewilderment of a ten-year-old Irish boy, Paddy Clarke, as he tries to make sense of his changing world.

Movies

Recently there have been many wonderful and deeply moving films that reflect Irish spirit, politics, and culture. Here are a few of the best:

The Commitments (1991), directed by Alan Parker. A brilliant film about a motley group of musicians who attempt to bring rhythm and blues music to the people of Dublin.

The Secret of Roan Inish (1994), directed by John Sayles. A movie for all ages, this is the heartwarming and magical story about a young girl, her family, and a legend. Filmed in a beautiful fishing village in County Donegal.

Michael Collins (1996). Directed by Neil Jordan, this is a powerful movie about the controversial life and death of Michael

Collins, who led the IRA against British rule in the early 1900s. ***Waking Ned Devine (1998).*** Funny and uplifting, this is the story of a lottery winner who dies of shock and his fellow Irish townsfolk who attempt to claim the money.

And don't forget the video version of *Angela's Ashes* (1999), also directed by Alan Parker, and John Huston's magnificent version of *The Dubliners* (1987).

Music

Celtic music includes the traditional music of the Celtic countries—Ireland, Scotland, Wales, Brittany (in France), Galicia (in Spain)—and areas that have come under their influence, such as the United States and the maritime provinces of Canada, as well as some newer music based on tradition from these countries. "Irish traditional music" is best understood as a very broad term that includes many different types of singing and instrumental music, music of many periods, as performed by Irish people in Ireland or outside it, and occasionally nowadays by people of other nationalities.

A one-hour weekly Celtic music show called "The Thistle & Shamrock" is currently broadcast on National Public Radio worldwide and featured on their online site. You can find out

When Irish Eyes Are Smiling

There's a tear in your eye and I'm wondering why,
For it never should be there at all.
With such power in your smile sure a stone you'd beguile,
So there's never a teardrop should fall.

When your sweet lilting laughter's like some fairy song
And your eyes twinkle bright as can be,
You should laugh all the while and all other times smile
and now smile a smile for me.

When Irish eyes are smiling,
Sure it's like a morning spring,
In the lilt of Irish laughter
You can hear the angels sing.

When Irish hearts are happy
All the world seems bright and gay,
And when Irish eyes are smiling,
Sure they'll steal your heart away.

more about Celtic music online at *www.ceolas.org,* which houses the largest collection of information on Celtic music and includes links to hundreds of related sites. Green Linnet Records, in the United States, has been recording Celtic music for the last twenty-five years. They have a catalog and Web site, *www.greenlinnet.com.*

A few of my favorite Celtic groups and musicians include the Chieftains, a Grammy Award-winning Irish traditional group that is known the world over (try *The Best of the Chieftains*); accordion player Sharon Shannon (*Each Little Thing* and *Out the Gap*); and Kevin Burke, one of the best traditional Irish fiddlers. Try his *In Concert* CD.

If you'd like to listen and sing along to traditional Irish vocal music, pick up a copy of *The Irish Tenors,* with John McDermott, Anthony Kearns, and Ronan Tynan. The CD, which includes a songbook, was recorded at the Royal Dublin Society Main Hall. It is a collection of Irish songs such as "Toora-Loora-Looral," "Danny Boy," and "When Irish Eyes Are Smiling."

After you've listened to the music, you might want to try playing the instruments. There are a couple of instruments that are relatively inexpensive and easy to play (unlike the harp and fiddle). They are the *bodhran* (pronounced "bo-rawn" or "bough-rawn"), a hand drum made of goatskin that is stretched across a round wooden frame and played with a wooden stick called a "tipper," and the tin whistle, which is a six-hole flute. These instruments can be found at most music stores, where you can also find guides for playing them.

Food

Once you're done with all the activities, it's time for a hearty meal served with brown bread and Irish butter—ideal for cool evenings. Desserts made with apples are common in Ireland. The recipe here is similar to an apple "crisp" or "crumble," with an Irish twist. Irish butter and McCann's Irish Oatmeal can be purchased at most grocery stores or at gourmet or specialty food outlets.

If you are looking for Irish cookbooks to expand your repertoire, I can recommend two: *The Irish Heritage Cookbook* by Margaret M. Johnson and *Irish Traditional Cooking* by Darina Allen. Both include hundreds of classic and more contemporary dishes sure to please. Johnson's book also features stories on unique items such as Irish honey, and a resource guide for buying them in the United States.

Potato Soup

2 lbs. potatoes	nutmeg to taste
1 large onion	salt and pepper to taste
4 tablespoons butter	1 cup milk
4 cups vegetable or chicken stock	1 tablespoon chives

Peel and cut the potatoes into cubes. Peel and finely slice the onion. Melt the butter in a large soup pot. Add the potatoes and onions, sauté on low heat for 10 minutes without turning the vegetables brown. Add the stock, salt, pepper, and nutmeg to taste. Cover and bring to a boil, stirring continuously. Reduce heat and simmer for 20 minutes, or until vegetables are soft, stirring occasionally. Stir in the milk and bring to a simmer on medium heat, stirring continuously so that milk doesn't curdle. Remove from heat. Serve with a sprinkling of chives. Serves 6.

Brown Bread

4 cups whole wheat flour	1½ teaspoons salt
2 cups white flour	1½ teaspoons baking soda
2 tablespoons butter	2 cups buttermilk, approximately

Mix the whole wheat flour thoroughly with the white flour. Incorporate the butter into the flour. Add the salt and baking soda. Make a well in the center and gradually mix in the buttermilk. You may need less, or more liquid—it depends on the absorbent quality of the flour. The dough should be soft but manageable.

Knead the dough in a mixing bowl into a ball with your floured hands. Place on a lightly floured baking sheet, and with the palm of your hand flatten out in a circle 1½ inches thick. With a knife dipped in flour, make a cross through the center of the bread so

that it will easily break into quarters when it is baked. Bake at 425°F for 25 minutes. Reduce the heat to 350°F and bake a further 15 minutes. If the crust seems too hard, wrap the baked bread in a damp tea cloth. Leave the loaf standing upright until it is cool. Makes 1 loaf.

Make Mine Guinness

The Irish are big drinkers and are known for several drinks that you might want to sample. Guinness, a delicious dark brew made with roasted malt, is the most famous stout in the world and is Ireland's national drink. Jameson and Bushmills are two famous Irish whiskeys. Irish Mist is an Irish liqueur that contains whiskey and honey, and Bailey's Irish Cream, another liqueur, is a concoction of whiskey and cream. Most towns and cities have an Irish pub that should be visited on your "trip" to Ireland, and most places serve the alcoholic beverages mentioned above. Or buy some at the liquor store and create your own pub at home.

Hot Oatmeal Apple Crumble

6 McIntosh or Granny Smith apples,
    peeled, cored, and sliced
$^3/_4$ cup butter
1 cup sugar
1 cup unbleached all-purpose flour

$^1/_4$ cup McCann's Quick Cooking Irish
    Oatmeal (found at most grocery stores)
$^1/_2$ teaspoon cinnamon
vanilla ice cream (optional)
Irish whiskey (optional)

Preheat oven to 375°F. Butter an 8-inch square baking dish. Arrange the apple slices on the bottom. Combine butter, sugar, and flour and blend until the mixture resembles coarse crumbs. Add the oatmeal and cinnamon and mix again. Spread evenly over the apples and bake until lightly browned (35–45 minutes). Allow to cool, and serve warm with vanilla ice cream and a splash of Irish whiskey on top, if desired. Serves 6.

—Sharon Donovan

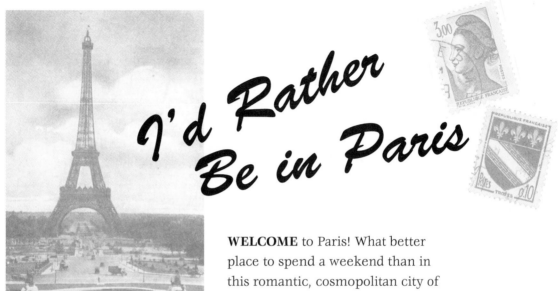

I'd Rather Be in Paris

WELCOME to Paris! What better place to spend a weekend than in this romantic, cosmopolitan city of lovers. And it's easy to replicate in your own home.

First, create a French café in the corner of a room by setting up little round tables surrounded by spindly-legged café chairs. Many of life's crucial

Setting the Scene

activities are carried out in French cafés—talking, reading, writing, eating, drinking—and this corner of your home can easily be the center of your Parisian weekend. To create an authentic feel, put crisp white tablecloths on your café tables topped with drinking glasses and bottles of Evian or Perrier water.

You can cover your walls inexpensively with the creations of French artists by getting a few posters. The Metropolitan Museum of Art in New York City has lots of posters that you can buy through their online store at *www.metmuseum.org/ store.* From the home page, click on "Posters," and you'll see a range of options: Impressionist and Post-Impressionist, European Art, Modern Art. Go with your own preferences to bring into your home the art of Monet, Degas, Gauguin, Renoir, Matisse, van Gogh, or Toulouse-Lautrec. Whereas Monet's work can bring you softly impressionistic images of the Seine River that runs through Paris, Toulouse-Lautrec's paintings will put bold and bright cabaret dancers at the Moulin Rouge onto your walls.

Although the official colors of the two countries are the same, the United States' "red, white, and blue" becomes "blue, white, and red" in France because that is the order of the three

colors on the French flag. If you want to decorate your home with the colors of France, you can easily create flags by using solid fabric or paper in these three colors and stitching or taping them together in one panel each of blue, white, and red, going from left to right. These are colors you might also use for streamers and other decorations.

COGNAC

Qualité Supérieure

★ ★ ★

Even the *Métro* (subway) signs in Paris are unique to that city, and when they are recreated in your home you might believe you are doing an authentic urban French stroll. Big Art Nouveau-style lettering of the full word *Métropolitain* appeared in wrought iron above subway stations in the early twentieth century to indicate entranceways to the world of transportation below the street, and some of those signs can still be seen in Paris. To replicate these signs, print large letters, each with a stylized Art Nouveau flourish, and shape the full word into an elegant arch to put above the doorways to the different rooms of your home.

For a final embellishment, go to a newspaper and magazine stand or shop and get some French publications to have lying around on tables in your transformed residence. Some easy publications to find will be *Le Monde* newspaper and *Elle* magazine.

Side Trip to Provence

The splendid beauty of the Provence region in the south of France can be attributed to many of its natural features, one of which is the lush array of flowers and herbs covering its gentle hills. You can bring the beauty and scents of the Provençal countryside into your weekend by filling baskets with the herbs of rosemary and thyme and putting dried lavender into tall vases. If the time of year is right, bring in some fresh sunflowers, which grow plentifully in Provence, and think of the human-like portraits of these large yellow flowers painted by Vincent van Gogh.

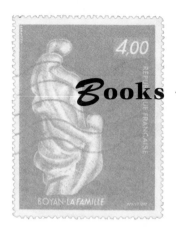

*B*ooks

Drop yourself right down into the middle of Paris by looking through the breathtaking pages of Robert Cameron's and Pierre Salinger's *Above Paris,* an astonishing book of aerial photographs. Cameron, a photographer, and Salinger, a journalist, in a single flight above the city of Paris captured views not available in any other book of photography. Its images are both sweepingly majestic, and, given the close range at which some of the photos were taken, surprisingly intimate. The gray *mansarde* rooftops that define the look of Paris as much as any other architectural feature are in full aerial view. The left and right banks of the Seine, linked by a succession of intricately detailed bridges, can be simultaneously appreciated from one vantage point. *Above Paris* brings together left and right, past and present, parks and residences, monuments and centuries-old buildings in a stunning way that is not possible from street-level views.

If you read Adam Gopnik's *Paris to the Moon: Essays on Contemporary Paris,* you will, in the comfy surroundings of your living room, come to understand why it is that an individual éclair, purchased at a French bakery with the intention of being eaten right away, will still be wrapped carefully, delicately, in doily-type paper that is securely and exquisitely held together by a starched white ribbon before it is handed to the customer. You will become attuned to the detailed attention given to everyday items and mundane locations that defines the "commonplace civility," to use Gopnik's term, that is most definitely at the heart of Parisian culture. Gopnik moved from New York to Paris with his wife, Martha, and young son, Luke, in 1995 and stayed for five years to write his "Paris Journals" feature for the *New Yorker* magazine, and the essays from that stint in Paris are at the core of this astute, penetrating, and enlightening book.

A Moveable Feast, Ernest Hemingway's memoir of his life in 1920s Paris, is an intimate portrait of the author and his many expatriate friends who together became known as "the lost generation." Gertrude Stein, Ezra Pound, James Joyce, F. Scott and Zelda Fitzgerald, Pablo Picasso, and others lived an intensely creative and intellectual Parisian life. As an integral player in this literary circle, "Papa" Hemingway came to know the personal details of an unparalleled group of writers and artists. In this slim and easily read memoir written toward the end of his life, he reveals those details together with his views of himself as a young writer and sentimental descriptions of the streets of Paris he knew and loved.

David Sedaris, whose quirky voice is widely recognized from his hilarious storytelling on National Public Radio, is one of the contemporary world's funniest writers. Get a copy of his book, *Me Talk Pretty One Day,* and bring some laughing out

loud into your Parisian weekend at home. The title of the book is Sedaris' painful mangling of French vocabulary and grammar, something he does in the bitingly witty tales that appear in the second half of his book about living as an American in Paris. You'll learn as much about Americans as about the French in his bull's-eye observations on the misfortune of being human, regardless of the culture you're from.

MINERVE·HÉRAULT

LA POSTE 1993
RÉPUBLIQUE
FRANÇAISE **4,20**

A totally fun novel that takes place in Paris is Diane Johnson's *Le Divorce.* Don't be fooled by the title; the book is written in English. The main character is the stylish, naïve, and indomitable Isabel Walker, a twenty-two-year-old Californian and recent dropout from film school, who discovers Paris while visiting her stepsister, Roxy, who is pregnant and going through a divorce from her aristocratic French husband. Paris gives Isabel a quick education in the ways of the world, from love and romance to money and murder. Paris in all its glory and singularities unfolds for us through Isabel's sassy slant on the world.

If children are celebrating your get-away-without-leaving-home weekend with you, some wonderful children's books will bring the world of Paris to them. A classic children's book, created by Ludwig Bemelmans in 1939, is *Madeline,* a story of a little French girl and her friends at Miss Clavel's French Boarding School. "In an old house in Paris that was covered in vines lived twelve little girls in two straight lines," begins the book, and we follow Madeline and the schoolgirls—all in matching outfits, topped with buoyant felt hats with perfectly flowing black ribbons—through the Parisian streets, past Notre Dame and the Opera House and the Tuileries gardens extending from the Louvre. (If *Madeline* is a hit with the kids this weekend, you might later want to introduce them to the five other books by Bemelmans that follow the self-assured redhead and her matched-wardrobe friends on their continuing adventures.)

Kay Thompson created another beloved children's character, Eloise, back in the 1950s. Whereas Madeline is French, Eloise is American—or, more precisely, a New Yorker fortunate enough to live in the elegant Plaza Hotel in the heart of Manhattan. After the first book, *Eloise,* won the hearts of children and parents across the United States, Thompson followed with *Eloise in Paris,* which lets us see the City of Light through the eyes of a very privileged and spunky little girl. Coming from the Plaza Hotel in New York City, nothing less than the Relais Bisson on the Quai des Grands Augustins, sitting majestically along the Seine, will do for Eloise. After settling into her new home (with thirty-eight pieces of luggage), she turns her attention to the world around her, and we see the sights of Paris through magical illustrations. In this enchanting book, children learn that Paris has, as Eloise eloquently puts it, "*beaucoup de* this and *beaucoup de* that, *beaucoup de* dog, *beaucoup de* cat."

For older children (ages nine and up), open up *Linnea in Monet's Garden.* After seeing impressionist artist Claude Monet's paintings in Paris, Linnea visits his magnificent gardens, still

Side Trip to Provence

A charming book that appeals to the dearly held fantasy of many people to live in the south of France, Peter Mayle's *A Year in Provence* presents that incomparable region of the world in its many colors. The writing is warm and fun and witty, and the descriptions of bountiful food—country bread, olive *tapenade,* pâté, earthy sauces, lemon sorbets— take you right into the heart of the delightful world that is Provence.

elaborately maintained today, in Giverny, a short distance from Paris. Beautiful color reproductions of Monet's work fill the pages, and readers learn about impressionist sensibilities and techniques through Linnea's young eyes.

France has contributed enormously to the world's finest literature, and you might go directly there this weekend by reading some classics, either in their original versions or in translation. Remember, the notion of the literary *salon* is a decidedly French one, and if your tastes are literary, you could fill your weekend with reading and discussing great works from French literature—intermingled with wonderful food and wine, for further sustenance. The literary possibilities are many, but here is a selective list of suggestions:

NOVELS

The Stranger *(L'étranger)* by Albert Camus
Madame Bovary by Gustave Flaubert
The Mandarins *(Les Mandarins)* by Simone de Beauvoir
The Lover *(L'amant)* by Marguerite Duras
Germinal by Emile Zola

PLAYS

The Would-Be Gentleman *(Le Bourgeois Gentilhomme)* by Molière
No Exit *(Huis Clos)* by Jean-Paul Sartre

POETRY

The Flowers of Evil *(Les Fleurs du Mal)* by Charles Baudelaire
The Drunken Boat *(Le Bateau Ivre)* by Arthur Rimbaud
   Long Ago and Not So Long Ago *(Jadis et Naguère)* by
Paul Verlaine

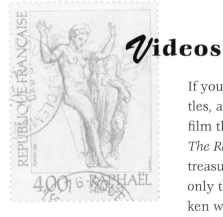

*V*ideos

If you don't know a word of French, don't like subtitles, and still want to watch an authentically French film that will carry you into the streets of Paris, rent *The Red Balloon* (1956). This brief and quite beautiful treasure by the late filmmaker Albert Lamorisse is only thirty-four minutes long and has only one spoken word in the entire film. The movie is both simple and profound, seeming to make large statements about childhood, loneliness, and friendship. The close-up views of iron lampposts, arched doorways, store window displays, gray rooftops, and detailed building facades that can be seen as the boy tries to catch up with the balloon, and it with him, show a historic Paris that still exists today. Lamorisse received both a Cannes Film Festival Grand Prize and an Academy Award for this gem. Images from the film were later used to create the book by Albert Lamorisse, also entitled *The Red Bal-loon.* The film and book are categorized as being for children, but their timelessness makes them wonderful to look at what-ever your age.

One of the most beautiful and melancholically romantic films of all times is *Les Enfants du Paradis (Children of Paradise,* 1946, English subtitles), directed by Marcel Carné. Set in nine-teenth-century Paris, this exquisite film follows a Parisian the-ater troupe and the love of a mime, Baptiste, for an actress, Garance. Baptiste, dressed in the full oversized costume of the Pierrot persona that suggests eternal childlike happiness is, un-derneath all the white folds and big buttons, suffering from the need to compete for Garance's attention, which is divided among Baptiste and three other suitors—an actor, an aristo-cratic count, and a thief. Astoundingly, this most sumptuous of films was created and filmed in Paris during Nazi occupation, while some of the filmmakers were being pursued by the Ger-man powers. Not only the film but its very making reveals the soaring possibilities of the human spirit.

A completely fun, colorful, and offbeat French film is *Les Parapluies de Cherbourg (The Umbrellas of Cherbourg,* 1964, Eng-lish subtitles), directed by Jacques Demy. What makes this film offbeat is that the dialogue is entirely sung rather than spoken, making it something of a cross between a musical and an operetta. Aside from its originality and playfulness, this film is worth watching for its unusual, almost hallucinogenic use of color. The story is about the life and loves of seventeen-year-old Geneviève (Catherine Deneuve), who lives with her mother, owner of an umbrella shop in the city of Cherbourg. This is the film that launched Catherine Deneuve into stardom. Since the dialogue is sung, if your French is good but not great, you might find this film easier to understand than more conventional ones. And, if not, subtitles are there to support you.

François Truffaut, master of the French New Wave movement that transformed cinema in the 1950s and 1960s, created *Jules et Jim (Jules and Jim,* 1962, English subtitles) starring the legendary Jeanne Moreau and considered by many to be the director's most poetic, most poignant, most accomplished film. This is the story of eternal friendship that will not be undone— even by a love triangle that sets two friends up to vie for their love for a woman. French film is known for its intense dialogue and philosophical discussions, and they are in full force in this film as the two men explore the meaning of love and friendship as the woman they love erratically moves back and forth between them. At turns light and frolicsome and aching and tragic, *Jules et Jim* is a *chef d'oeuvre* of French film.

Another film that emerged from the French New Wave is *Hiroshima, Mon Amour (Hiroshima, My Love,* 1959, English subtitles), directed by Alain Resnais and written by the brilliant French novelist Marguerite Duras. When a French woman connects romantically with a Japanese man in Hiroshima while she is in Japan to do some filming, she is haunted by memories of an earlier love—between her and a German soldier during Germany's occupation of France—a scandal which, when exposed during that earlier time, had brought shame to her and her family. Her Japanese lover suffers from his own troubled history. The complex film, which moves frequently between past and present, France and Japan, and actual time and memories, explores the traumatic after-effects of war and the potential healing that can come from connection with another person.

If you would rather watch something light, turn to *An American in Paris* (1951), full with the happy music of George Gershwin and the spriteful dancing of Gene Kelly. The movie was made on MGM lots rather than in Paris itself, but you'll see a recreated Paris in every scene. There is a storyline to this movie, but the plot is incidental to the music and dancing. On the receiving end of many Academy Awards after it was first released, *An American in Paris* is the source of continuing musical favorites, such as "I Got Rhythm" and "Our Love Is Here to Stay."

Side Trip to Provence

If you want to spend part of your weekend in Provence, there are four lusciously beautiful films based on Marcel Pagnol's novels you could turn to, all showing the breathtaking countryside of the south of France. *Jean de Florette* (*Jean de Florette*, 1987, English subtitles), starring the renowned French actors Gérard Depardieu, Yves Montand, and Daniel Auteuil, is about a farmer in 1920s Provence whose trust causes him to lose his land to a covetous neighbor; the seamlessly continuing sequel, *Manon des Sources* (*Manon of the Spring*, 1987, English subtitles), follows Jean de Florette's daughter, played by Emmanuelle Béart, as she grows into womanhood and tries to avenge the wrong done to her father. Another pair of movies adapted from Pagnol's work and set in the Provençal countryside is *La Gloire de Mon Père* (*My Father's Glory*) and its sequel, *Le Château de Ma Mère* (*My Mother's Castle*), both launched in 1991 with English subtitles. Drawing directly from Pagnol's personal boyhood experiences in Provence, these gorgeous and charming films celebrate family, warmth, and the simple joys a visit to the country can bring.

Music

Of course you need to listen to Edith Piaf the moment your Parisian weekend kicks off. Hers has been called "the voice of the sparrow," and her songs are the very definition of what is French. You won't have any trouble finding Edith Piaf CDs—she is loved the world around.

You might put on the CD entitled *Edith Piaf: Her Greatest Recordings (1935–1943),* on which you'll find classics like "L'Etranger" ("The Stranger") and "Fais-moi Valser" ("Make Me Waltz"). Piaf's style immediately conjures up French cabaret scenes.

Another cabaret singer, and a captivating star of the Parisian world mid-twentieth century, is Josephine Baker. Born an American in St. Louis, Baker had already made a name for herself in Paris while in her teens. The beautiful performer sang in both French and her native English, and her shows at the Folies Bergères cabaret were salty, humorous, and sensuously seductive. The CD *J'ai Deux Amours: Mon Pays et Paris (I Have Two Loves: My Country and Paris)* will fill your living room with Paris.

Born in Belgium, Jacques Brel came to know great success in France through his many performances there, and, despite his Belgian roots, his songs have become as much a part of traditional French music as any other. He is known for his witty, ironic, and sometimes irreverent and politically charged lyrics as well as for his romantic ballads, of which the aching and heartbreaking "Ne Me Quitte Pas'" ("Don't Leave Me") is considered by some to be the most beautiful French song of all times. There are lots of Brel CDs to choose from, but you might go right to *Ne Me Quitte Pas,* which includes, in addition to the title track, such favorites as "Quand On N'a Que L'amour" ("When You Have Only Love"), "Les Biches" ("Sweethearts"), and "On N'oublie Rien" ("Nothing Is Forgotten").

Particularly if yours is a romantic weekend, fill the air with music from *Paris My Love,* a compilation of traditional Parisian love songs. You'll find Edith Piaf and Josephine Baker here, and also the swooning sounds of Maurice Chevalier and music for lovers from Jean Sablon and Lucienne Boyer and Jean Gabin.

If you are looking for a more contemporary French scene, try pop musician Patricia Kaas. Kaas came onto the stage in the early 1990s, and her popularity has been escalating since, even crossing the Atlantic Ocean to be embraced by many music lovers in the United States. Kaas' voice is capable of anything, it seems, ranging from sultry to soaring, erotic to electrifying. Try to get the *Je Te Dis Vous* CD.

The band is no longer around, but the music of Mano Negra continues to rock the house. A strong Latin sensibility informs the band's name, yet, make no mistake, Mano Negra is a French group—with multicultural ethno-punk sounds. The group, whose music was fueled by reggae tempos, hip-hop rhythms, and Latin-Cuban beats, disbanded in the early 1990s, but new CD compilations continue to be released. Put on *The Best of Mano Negra* and experience a new version of Things French.

France's best rapper is unquestionably MC Solaar. When rap first emerged in the United States, it was thought by many to be a uniquely English-language phenomenon—certainly not an art form that could migrate to the more flowery French language. MC Solaar has proved the purists amazingly wrong—creating powerful, sensual raps that are in their way as poetic as anything created by Baudelaire. Listen to the *Prose Combat* CD and hear the French language spoken with the sensibility of a modern-day intellectual urban poet.

ood

Breakfast is a much simpler meal in France than it is in North America (at least when we actually stop to have breakfast). Bread with *beurre* and *confiture* (butter and jelly) and perhaps a *croissant* are often the center of the meal, with a big steaming bowl-like cup of *café au lait*— or steamed milk or hot chocolate for non-coffee drinkers.

Get fresh breads and croissants at your best French bakery in town, and make *café au lait* with equal parts coffee and steamed milk. The French have been known to sneak a little chocolate with their breakfast, either in the form of *pain au chocolat,* which is essentially a chocolate-filled croissant, or straight from the source with a piece or two of chocolate with their bread.

For lunch, you might put down the books, turn off the videos, and temporarily stop the music to get outside for a French-style picnic. Bring along a brightly colored tablecloth for the ground and pack into a basket a *baguette* or two, some cheese, perhaps Camembert or Gruyère, some apples, oranges, and pears, and a bottle of Evian water and/or a good red wine from the Burgundy region toward the north of France, the Bordeaux region toward the Atlantic coast, or the Rhone region in Provence. If you didn't have chocolate at breakfast, you might slip a Toblerone bar into the basket. Don't forget a knife for the cheese and fruit, a corkscrew for the wine, and lots of napkins. On your way back home, stop at a cozy café for an espresso or herbal tea; some French favorites are chamomile and verveine.

If you opt to stay home for lunch, you can go simple with a veggie-filled crèpe (zucchini and mushrooms are especially good) or a *Salade Niçoise* (see recipe).

In the mid-afternoon, you might want to take the edge off after lunch and before dinner. French-style snacks that you can find in some French bakeries and specialty stores include *marrons glacés,* which are soft, candied chestnuts, and *flan,* a kind of thick custard.

The French do not generally drink before-dinner cocktails. Instead, open the bottle of wine that you will be drinking with dinner and begin enjoying it before the meal begins.

French diners are more inclined than their American counterparts to drink after-dinner drinks. Cognac is a kind of brandy from the Cognac Valley in France, about 200 miles southwest of Paris, and it is served only after a meal—often with great ceremony. It is said that all cognac is brandy, but not all brandy is cognac, thus putting cognac on a higher plane of appreciation from other brandies. A particularly French after-dinner drink is Calvados, an apple brandy that is, in essence, distilled hard cider. Not any apple brandy can be called Calvados, however—only the apple brandy that is produced in Normandy, the French *département* that is at the very heart of France's apple-growing region and where over 800 different kinds of apples are grown. The French appreciate Calvados not only for its crisp and fruity taste but for what they believe are its digestion-enhancing attributes.

Following are recipes for *Salade Niçoise* as well as a suggested dinner of mussels in white wine, asparagus over toasted brioche, and chocolate mousse. Select a French white wine, a

Beer? In France?

People, of course, think of wine when they think of France, but did you know that France has more than 1,000 breweries? Its best-known beer is Kronenbourg, whose main brewery and headquarters are in Strasbourg, in the Alsace region of France that shares a border with Germany. You won't find Kronenbourg beer in grocery stores, but you might find it in specialty stores and on the beer menu of some American bars.

Chardonnay or a Sauvignon Blanc, to accompany the meal, and end with a lovely glass of cognac or Calvados.

To experiment with other meals and recipes, you have a legion of French cookbooks to choose from. *The Food Lover's Guide to France, The Food Lover's Guide to Paris,* and *Bistro Cooking* are all by award-winning restaurant critic Patricia Wells. Julia Child has several French cookbooks: *Mastering the Art of French Cooking* (Volumes 1 and 2) and *The French Chef Cookbook.* For some lighter French meals, try *Jacques Pépin's Simple and Healthy Cooking.* And, for their stunning design as well as their recipes, take a look at *France: The Beautiful Cookbook* and *Provence: The Beautiful Cookbook.*

Salade Nicoise

1 7-oz. can tuna packed in
    water, drained
1 head romaine lettuce, washed
    and dried
1 lb. tiny potatoes, boiled until
    tender, thinly sliced
1 lb. green beans, trimmed and cut
    into thirds, steamed until tender
6 scallions, chopped
1 red bell pepper, thinly sliced
5 medium tomatoes, cut into wedges

½ cup whole oil-cured black olives
4 hard-boiled eggs, sliced
1 2-oz. can anchovies, drained
1 tablespoon finely minced mixed herbs,
    including parsley, tarragon, rosemary
3 cloves garlic, chopped finely
¼ teaspoon Dijon mustard
¼ cup red wine vinegar
Salt and pepper to taste
½ cup olive oil

Separate and flake the tuna.

    Put the salad ingredients in a large bowl by layer, in this order: lettuce, potatoes, green beans, scallions, pepper, tomatoes, tuna, olives, eggs, anchovies, herbs.

    To prepare the vinaigrette, whisk together the garlic, mustard, vinegar, salt, and pepper. Add the oil and continue whisking until thoroughly blended. Toss the salad gently with the vinaigrette and serve immediately. Serves 6.

Moules à la Marinière

(MUSSELS IN WHITE WINE SAUCE)

2 tablespoons unsalted butter

3 cloves garlic, thinly sliced

2 shallots, thinly sliced

3 lbs. medium or large black mussels,
    rinsed, scrubbed, and debearded

3 sprigs fresh thyme

2 bay leaves

2 tablespoons heavy cream

½ cup dry white wine

freshly ground black pepper to taste

salt to taste

Melt the butter in a large pot over medium heat, add the garlic and shallots, cover the pot, and cook for 1 minute. Add the mussels, thyme, and bay leaves, re-cover the pot, and cook about 1 minute, until the mussels begin to open. Add the heavy cream, wine, and black pepper. Cover and cook for 1 minute. Remove from heat. Taste the liquid and, if necessary, add salt to taste.

To serve, be sure to discard any mussels that have not opened, divide the remaining mussels into four soup bowls, and pour the liquid over the mussels. Diners should feel free to use their hands to pick up the mussels and remove the seafood from the shell. Serves 4.

Brioche aux Asperges

(ASPARAGUS OVER TOASTED BRIOCHE)

This really should be made with fat asparagus.

2 lbs. asparagus

water to cover

3 tablespoons butter

salt and pepper to taste

4 pieces brioche or egg bread,
    sliced 1-inch thick

Preheat the broiler.

In a single layer, place the asparagus in a large saucepan. (Use two saucepans if yours are small and won't fit the asparagus in a single layer.) Add water to almost, but not quite, cover the asparagus. Add butter, salt, and pepper. Bring to a boil over high heat. Cook about 8 minutes, until the asparagus is tender to the bite.

Toast the brioche or egg bread in the broiler. Place one slice of brioche on each of 4 plates and layer the asparagus spears on top. Spoon over the juices and serve immediately. Serves 4.

Mousse au Chocolat

(CHOCOLATE MOUSSE)

8 oz. bittersweet chocolate, broken
    into pieces

2 teaspoons vanilla

8 tablespoons unsalted butter, cut
    up into pieces

1/2 cup sugar, preferably superfine

8 egg yolks

5 egg whites

In the top of a double boiler over gently boiling water, put the chocolate and vanilla. Stir until melted, then remove from heat. Add the butter and stir until melted.

In a large bowl, beat the sugar and egg yolks until thick. Add the chocolate.

In a separate bowl, beat the egg whites until stiff. Add about a third of the egg whites to the chocolate mixture and beat until well mixed. Gradually fold in the remaining egg whites, and, this time, mix gently rather than vigorously. Blend well, but do not overmix.

Pour the mixture into a large serving bowl and cover with plastic wrap. Refrigerate at least 7 hours before serving. Serves 8.

—Leslie Berriman

Touring Tuscany

Setting the Scene

TUSCANY conjures up images of red roofs, green pastures, low hills, beautiful coastline, and fabulous food! To create this beauty for a weekend, first soften your living areas; use as much natural sunlight as possible—lighten up on the fluorescents. Create a simple, open area within your home, moving away unnecessary knick-knacks, chairs, and tables. Use pillows, family photos, bowls of fruit, and vases of wildflowers for decoration. Go for as many reds and yellows as possible; poppies and sunflowers make wonderfully authentic decorations. Wear long skirts and peasant blouses or black pants and white shirts for a truly Tuscan touch.

If possible, create an open area in your backyard or balcony for a small table and chairs for dining *al fresco.* If this is not possible, make a luxurious eating area within your home. Use bright tablecloths and napkins, candles, and potted herbs and other small plants as scenery. As Tuscans spend much of their time with food, whether eating or in preparation to dine, your eating area is one of the most important parts of this armchair adventure!

Inexpensive calendars, posters, and postcards of Tuscan artists would make a nice background to any scene you decide to set. Michelangelo, Cellini, Fra Angelico, da Vinci, Botticelli, and Fiorentino are just a few of the Tuscan artists whose artworks have been reproduced in many forms. Pisa, Chianti, Florence, San Gimignano, and Siena are some of the most photographed cities in Tuscany, providing breathtaking landscapes and architecture for painters and photographers alike.

For a quiet weekend at home in Tuscany, make sure to leave time for walks in the neighborhood park, or even a drive out into the nearest countryside. For an evening's entertainment, spend some time outside under the night sky. Astronomer Galileo Galilei was from Tuscany, and an evening outside, with a bottle of wine and some good cheeses and fruit, would be the best way to commune with the heavens Galileo opened up for us. (For a good read on Galileo, get *Galileo's Daughter: A Historical Memoir of Science, Faith and Love* by Dava Sobel. In it, Sobel tells the story of the famous scientist and his illegitimate daughter, Sister Maria Celeste.)

*B*ooks

Unless you've been asleep since the 1980s, you've probably heard of *Under the Tuscan Sun: At Home in Italy* and *Bella Tuscany* by Frances Mayes. Mayes bought a home in Tuscany, and writes about the joys and frustrations of fixing and repairing in a new country, as well as the life of the people surrounding her new home. Filled with recipes and descriptions of Tuscan living, both titles are great for getting the feel of Tuscany.

There are many incredible illustrated books on Tuscany available for leisurely perusing. Here are some of the best:

From "The Great Museums of the World" series comes *Uffizi: Florence.* This book of the magnificent artworks of the Uffizi Museum in Florence covers the artists and the history of each particular piece. It's a good introduction to the magnificence of art in Italy, as well as the many fine artists of Tuscany.

In Tuscany, by Frances Mayes with Edward Mayes, is a wonderfully thorough book of essays and photos celebrating the abundant pleasures of life as it is lived in this region at home and in restaurants, festivals, feasts, in the kitchen and outdoors. Recipes are scattered throughout the book, with a concentration in the section entitled *La Cucina.* Mayes' descriptions of the countryside are enough to make you feel the dust of the road in your nostrils and hear the sound of dry wheat rasping in the wind, and with its wonderful photographs this is the book to keep out on your table long after your "trip" is over.

The Stones of Florence by Mary McCarthy, with photos by Evelyn Hofer, is a pictorial look at the beautiful city of Florence, while *The Most Beautiful Villages of Tuscany,* by James Bently, with photos by Hugh Palmer, focuses on thirty-six towns and villages around Tuscany. It truly evokes the beauty of the land.

Matthew Spender writes on art, history, and culture in *Within Tuscany: Reflections on a Time and Place.* A captivating book that offers readers a personal glimpse into the life and times of a man and his family in the Tuscan countryside. Another book that well evokes the beauty and simplicity of Tuscany is *A Tuscan Childhood,* by Kinta Beevor.

The Tuscan Year: Life and Food in an Italian Valley is a complete look at a year in the life of a family in Tuscany, with the main focus on food and feasts. Written by Elizabeth Romer and arranged month by month, *The Tuscan Year* looks at the ancient way of life and cuisine of Tuscany, each chapter punctuated with well-directed recipes.

Poetry lovers should consider Christopher Ryan's translation of *Michelangelo: The Poems.* A wonderful surprise, this book

Italian Phrases to Toss Around

Per favore = Please

Andiamo = Let's go

Grazie = Thank you

Ciao = Hello

Arrivederci = Good-bye

Buongiorno = Good day

Buono = Good; Okay

Salute! = Cheers

of poetry by Michelangelo lets readers have a new glimpse into the artist's mind. From sonnets to madrigals, Michelangelo Buonarroti wrote on love, art, beauty, death, and time. A wonderful read, with the Italian and English translations side by side. Or consider reading Dante Alighieri's *Divine Comedy* or *Vita Nuova* out loud. Through his work, this native of Florence established Tuscan as the literary language of Italy.

If you are in the mood for a novel, consider *War in the Val d'Oricia* by Iris Origo, which is the experience of a woman and her husband in World War II Italy, their children's shelter, and the march across the Tuscan countryside to safety.

Or how about Irving Stone's *The Agony and the Ecstasy*? This biographical novel of Michelangelo is both fascinating and factual. This is a long book, although well worth the time it takes to read it, encompassing the history of Italy, the popes, the powerful Medici family during Michelangelo's lifetime, as well as the beauty of Italy. Certain chapters give compelling descriptions of Tuscany.

Videos

There are so many films about this beautiful
part of the world. Here are some of the best:

Romola (1924). In Renaissance Florence, Tito, a
young man pretending to be a scholar, wins the
admiration of a blind man looking for someone
to finish his scholarly work. The blind man has a
beautiful daughter named Romola, whom he
wishes to marry to Tito. Romola marries Tito for
her father's sake, and regrets this decision when
Tito joins the new government (after the Medicis are forced out).
Tito's actions in the government incur the wrath of Romola and
the people, and he is killed by an angry mob.

The Night of the Shooting Stars (1982). In Italian, with English
subtitles, this story set in the summer of 1944 captures the beauty
of the Tuscan countryside and its people. A group of villagers aban-
don their homes in search of approaching American GIs. The story
is seen through the eyes of a six-year-old girl.

A Room with a View (1986). A young Englishwoman (Helena
Bonham Carter) falls in love in Florence, and is forced to choose
between convention and passion. The beginning of this film (the

first 40 minutes) offers beautiful shots of the Tuscan countryside and the interior of Santa Croce, enhanced by the music of Puccini. The opening credits begin with an unforgettable aria from *Gianni Schicchi,* "O mio babbino caro."

Cinema Paradiso (1990). A young boy in a small Italian village is befriended by the projectionist at the movie theater. As he grows up he learns to love films and is encouraged by his good friends to pursue his dream of one day making movies. Although this movie does not take place in Tuscany, this close look at the Italian people and life in a small Italian town should not be missed.

Taking the Waters

Terme di Saturnia is an ancient spa in southern Tuscany, believed to have been created by an angry Saturn. The legend is that Saturn, irritated at the mortals traipsing the earth, threw down a lightning rod. When the rod hit the earth, warm sulfurous water gushed from the crater of a volcano. These baths, which have pre-Etruscan walls and Roman structures, are filled with millions of tiny bubbles and healing warmth. Take a moment to create your own mini-spa time. Take a long, hot bath using your favorite mineral treatments; this is the time to try mud packs, algae masks, and Dead Sea salts!

Il Ciclone (1996). Levante lives in a small city near Florence, and he feels his life is a little dull. The day the twister *(il ciclone)* arrives (a bus with six Spanish flamenco dancers) Levante and his family life become a part of the storm.

Life Is Beautiful (La Vita e Bella, 1998). Filmed in the Tuscan town of Arezzo, this film directed by Roberto Benigni is a love story of Guido (Roberto Benigni) and Dora (Nicoletta Brashi) in World War II Italy. Occasionally dark, when focusing upon the racial laws of Italy and the concentration camp in which the family is sent, this film has beautiful scenes of the Italian countryside and is ultimately uplifting in its message.

Tea with Mussolini (1999). Pseudo-biographical tale from the early life of director Franco Zeffirelli. This movie looks at the life of a bastard son of an Italian businessman, whose mother has died and is raised by an Englishwoman (Joan Plowright) in pre–WWII Mussolini Italy. Living in an English community in Florence presided over by an ex-diplomat's wife (Maggie Smith), he and the Englishwomen live a sheltered existence that they believe is guaranteed protection by Mussolini himself in a tea reception that Smith holds with Il Duce. Judy Dench and Cher also star in this colorful film with shots of Florence and San Gimignano.

Up the Villa (2000). On a vacation near Florence in 1938, a penniless English widow considers the marriage proposal of an aging

British aristocrat. After a good deed results in tragedy, she must choose between dependability and love, her reputation and her feelings.

Music

The music of Tuscany is primarily opera, so if you are looking to have an authentic experience, you should give this musical form a hearing. Italian opera centers around four Italian cities, one of which is Florence. Florentines, in the last decade of the sixteenth century, created a new style of singing, called *stile rappresentativo* (theater style), which became one of the earliest forms of opera. *Euridice,* written by Rinuccini, Peri, and Caccini in 1660, and *Orfeo,* written by Claudio Monteverde, are two of the most important early operas from Italy. Monteverde also wrote the *Fifth Book of Madrigals* and *L'Incoronazione di Poppea.*

Giacomo Puccini, born in the Tuscan town of Lucca, is one of the most masterful and passionate composers of all time. His works have touched the hearts of millions; in fact, opera star Mirella Freni never performed the title role of *Madama Butterfly* because she said it made her too emotional: "I tried to do it once. In rehearsal I cried so much the pianist started crying too."

Puccini wrote twelve operas, including *Turandot, La Bohème, Tosca, Madama Butterfly,* and *Gianni Schicchi.* The complete works are usually found in local libraries or music stores, and the more famous pieces are found on compilation works: "Nessun Dorma" *(Turandot);* "Si. Mi Chiamano Mimi" *(La Bohème);* "Amore o grillo" *(Madama Butterfly);* "Recondita armonia" *(Tosca);* "Un bel di" *(Madama Butterfly);* and "Che gelida manina" *(La Bohème).*

A newcomer on the opera scene, Andrea Bocelli is from the small town of Lajatico in Tuscany. His hit albums include *Romanza, Sogno, Nights in Tuscany, Arie Sacre, Per Amore,* and renditions of Verdi and *La Bohème.* Libraries and music stores carry most of his music, and his Web site, *www.bocellionline. com,* lists albums not found in the United States.

If you'd rather avoid opera, consider music by Luigi Boccherini. He was an influential but little known Tuscan composer whose work spans from string quintets and symphonies to cello concertos and guitar pieces. Some nice collections are *Cello Concerto #2, 3, 9,* and *10, The Best of Boccherini, Boccherini: The Guitar Quintets,* and *Luige Boccherini: 28 Symphonies.*

Food

The midday meal is the main one of the day and begins with a first course (*primo*) consisting of pasta, :sotti, or polenta dishes. Next is *secondo,* the meat or fish courses accompanied by a vegetable or salad, followed by fruit or cheese and coffee. On Sundays and special days there is an *antipasto* before the *primo,* and two or three different *secondi* and a dessert.

Tuscan food is simple, requiring only fresh ingredients and basic cookery; a large saucepan, long-handled spoons, a large colander, and frying pans and small pans for sauces.

A few good cookbooks to try out are *The Tuscan Year* by Elizabeth Romer; *Tuscany: Authentic Recipes from the Provinces of Tuscany* by Lorenza de Medici; *Classic Tuscany: The Tuscan Cookbook* by Wilma Pezzini; and the *Italian Farmhouse Cookbook* by Susan Herrmann Loomis.

The menu here offers two antipasti, a soup, a pasta dish, a chicken main course, and a side dish of white beans. Finish off with fruit, if you still have room!

Pomodori Fritti

(FRIED TOMATOES)

Fried tomatoes aren't only a southern U.S. dish, but are a popular Tuscan favorite too. The Italian version, usually served as an antipasto, is made with ripe tomatoes.

4 medium-sized firm tomatoes
½ cup corn meal
1 cup olive oil

½ cup fresh grated mozzarella
4 small sprigs fresh basil

Choose firm, barely ripe tomatoes and cut into wedges. Roll the tomato pieces in the corn meal. Heat the olive oil over high heat until smoking. Plunge the tomato pieces into the smoking olive oil and cook quickly, until the surface is a light golden color. Drain on paper towels and remove to a plate. Top with fresh mozzarella and garnish with basil. Serves 4.

Frittata di Cipollo

(ONION FRITTATA)

4 eggs
1 onion

2 tablespoons olive oil
salt and pepper to taste

Beat the eggs in a small bowl and season with the salt and pepper. Set aside.

Slice the onion into thin slices. In an omelet or thick-bottomed pan, heat the oil over medium-low heat. Add the onions. When the onion has become transparent, but before it has started to brown, raise the heat under the pan and spread the onion evenly over the

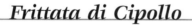

bottom of the pan. Pour the eggs in the pan and jiggle the pan to distribute the eggs, but do not stir.

Lower the heat and let the eggs cook slowly. When the eggs are firm on the bottom, slide the frittata gently out of the pan onto a plate. Raise the heat again, adding more oil if necessary, then tip the frittata, raw side down, back into the pan. Cook for a few minutes to set the bottom into a crust. To serve, put the frittata on a plate and cut into wedges. Serves 4.

Minestrone di Verdura

1 large onion
2 large carrots
2 stalks celery
2 large potatoes, peeled
¼ cup olive oil
1 15½-oz. can cooked white beans, drained

1 15½-oz. can peeled tomatoes, crushed
3½ cups beef, chicken or vegetable stock, approximately
6–8 fresh sprigs fresh parsley
salt and pepper to taste

Finely dice the onions, carrots, celery, and potatoes. Heat the oil in a large saucepan and add the diced vegetables. Cook over medium heat until softened but not browned. Add the beans, then mix in the tomatoes. Add the parsley and 2 cups of stock. There should be just enough stock to barely cover the vegetables. Season the soup with salt and pepper to taste. Simmer the soup until the vegetables are tender. Serves 6.

SPAGHETTI HOUSE

Spaghetti al Salsa di Pomodoro Crudo

(SPAGHETTI WITH FRESH TOMATO SAUCE)

This is a dish that is only worth doing if you have really good, juicy tomatoes, homegrown preferred. And the longer it sits around the better, so start in the morning if you plan to have this for dinner.

8 small tomatoes

½ cup green olive oil

1 sprig fresh basil, leaves roughly
    torn, or ¼ cup dry

2 cloves garlic, peeled and bruised

salt and pepper to taste

14 oz. spaghetti

Skin the tomatoes with a sharp knife. Cut the tomatoes roughly and place in a bowl. Include any tomato juice. Add the garlic and basil. Pour the olive oil into the bowl and mix thoroughly. Place on a counter and let sit until dinner. Do not put into the refrigerator or it will lose flavor.

When you are ready to eat, cook the spaghetti according to package directions. Drain well, then place in a serving bowl. Remove the garlic cloves from the sauce and add salt and pepper to taste. Pour the sauce onto the pasta, mixing well. Serves 4.

Pollo at Diavolo

This is a dish that can be made on a barbecue if the weather permits. Adjust the red pepper depending on your preference for spiciness.

½ cup olive oil

1 large lemon

1 tablespoon crushed red pepper, approximately

salt and pepper to taste

1 cut-up frying chicken

Pour the olive oil and lemon juice into a dish large enough to hold the chicken. Add the crushed red pepper, salt, and pepper, and stir. Place the chicken in the marinade for at least 1 hour, turning several times.

Grill the chicken for about 10 minutes on each side on a barbecue, basting occasionally with leftover marinade. Serves 4.

Fagioli all'uccellotto

(WHITE BEANS IN TOMATO SAUCE)

This makes a lovely side dish with bruschetta or just large chunks of bread.

14 oz. dried white beans

2 tablespoons olive oil

3 cloves garlic

4 fresh sage leaves, or 1 teaspoon dry

salt and pepper to taste

1 15½-oz. can peeled tomatoes,
    drained and chopped

To cook the white beans, soak them overnight in plenty of cold water. Rinse them, put them in a clean pan and cover them with fresh water. Cook them over a medium flame until they are tender (this should take about an hour and a half). Salt them during the last 15 minutes of cooking. Drain.

In a large pan, heat the olive oil over medium heat and add the garlic, sage, salt, and pepper. Cook, stirring constantly, until garlic is golden, about 3 minutes. Add the beans and tomatoes. Simmer for 15 minutes. Serves 4.

— *Teresa Coronado*

The Glorious Grape

Tuscany is well known for its fabulous wines. The most important red wines are from the *sangiovese* grapes, including the 1994 Brunello di Montalcino (Uccelliera); 1994 Carmingnano (Villagiachi); 1997 Chianti Classico (La Cinciole). The white wines of San Gimignano are known for their crisp and dry qualities; check out the 1997 Vernaccia di San Gimignano "Vigna Casanuova" and "Crete Nere." Other Tuscan wines include 1998 Piccini Chianti, 1998 Paradiso Vernaccia di San Gimignano, 1998 Giacomo Mori Chianti Colli Senesi, and 1997 Collelungo Chianti Classico.

Glorious Greece

Setting the Scene

THERE are more than 2,000 Greek isles. Not all of them are inhabited, of course, but even so, that's a lot of islands to choose from for your fantasy. You can dream of being pampered in a luxurious upscale resort with yachts and expensive shops nearby; of hiking on fragrant deserted hills overlooking the ocean; of scrambling among ancient ruins, with crumbling temples and columns; of sunning yourself alone on a quiet black-sand beach, or joining others on a strip of sand that's like a perpetual party; of seeking out small Greek Orthodox churches with beautiful icons; or eating a simple meal at a *taverna* that's right beside the dock of a bustling fishing village.

When I think of the Greek Isles, I think first of the colors: brilliant white and bright blues—the sky blue of roofs and the sapphire blue of the Aegean. To bring that feeling into your home, decorate with those colors if you can; use cushion covers, drape shawls, display blue glass vases. Fling the curtains wide to let in as much light as possible. Open photo books to blue and white scenes and leave them on the coffee table for leafing though. If you have any embroidered peasant shirts tucked away, dig them out and wear them.

To simulate the Greek countryside, if you have herbs growing in your back yard, pick a bunch and put them in a vase as you would cut flowers, and occasionally crush a leaf between your fingers and smell the aroma; rosemary, mint, basil, oregano, or bay would be especially apt. Beside your herbs, display a large bowl of bright yellow lemons.

The Greek Isles have been inhabited for more than 3,000 years, and they provide a background for some of the elaborate mythology made famous by Homer. The Greek people are proud of their rich classical history, so why don't you get out your atlas and locate some of the islands where the gods played? Just a few examples: Delos, the birthplace of Apollo;

It's Greek to Me

When you think of the Venus de Milo, do you associate her only with the Louvre? It's easy to forget her origins. She was created on Melos, one of the Cylades islands, around 100 B.C.E. There are conflicting stories about her unearthing in 1820; some say she was discovered already broken in an underground cavern, others that she was found among a pile of rocks about to be sent to a lime kiln for crushing; others that when found she was complete, and lost her arms in transit to France.

The Greek island of Chios provided one of the best-known sights in Venice: the quartet of bronze horses that stand over the main doors of St. Mark's Church. The ancient sculptures were looted by Constantine the Great in around 330 when he conquered the island, and were taken to his new city of Constantinople. There they stayed until their move to Venice in 1204. (Their heads were cut off to make them easier to transport.) Then in 1797, when Napoleon invaded Venice, he took a fancy to the horses and sent them to Paris, to be returned slightly damaged twenty years later by the French government.

Most lists of famous Spanish painters include the great Renaissance artist El Greco, but of course the name tells it all . . . he was Greek! Born in 1541 on the isle of Crete, Domenikos Theotokopoulos never forgot his roots, and always signed his paintings with his full name, in Greek letters.

Δομενικο

Θεοτοκοπουλο

Skiros, where Achilles was raised disguised as a girl; Ikaria, where Ikarus drowned when his wings of wax melted; and Ithaka, the home that Odysseus spent so many years striving to return to. The myths are fascinating, complex, and interwoven, and the islands played host to many of them.

If you have any Greek Orthodox icons, put them in a prominent place. And to really get in the mood, buy some of the best Greek olives, the Kalamata from the Peloponesos, and put out dishes of them for snacking all weekend long. Why not also buy a bottle of ouzo, the anise-flavored Greek liqueur? It's traditionally drunk straight, but some like it better on the rocks—then it will turn from clear to milky white before your eyes. For those of you willing to pull out all the stops, buy some cheap glasses, and at the end of the evening drink your ouzo, then hurl the glasses into the fireplace!

Easter in Greece

There is no bigger occasion on the Greek calendar than Easter. This religious celebration of resurrection and rebirth coincides with the arrival of spring, when in the countryside fields of red poppies emerge, a joyous time of nature's rebirth. Garlands of flowers are made on Good Friday, and first thing on Easter Saturday food preparation begins: a traditional soup with lambs innards is made; eggs are hard boiled and dyed crimson to represent the blood of Christ; Easter bread into which crimson eggs are pressed is baked; cookies and pastries round out the celebration. After midnight mass on Saturday, the first round of Easter feasting begins, as the traditional lamb soup and dyed eggs are eaten. Early on Sunday morning, in courtyards and village squares, charcoal is lit for the roasting of the traditional lamb or goat. It is rubbed with oregano and mint, then secured on a spit. Through the morning while it's cooking people eat snacks or visit friends. Some will play a game with more of the crimson boiled eggs, wherein each person takes an egg and tries to crack the egg of another (the cracking of the shell symbolizing breaking out of the tomb). The last person in the group whose egg remains unbroken is ensured good luck. The elaborate feast of lamb and side dishes is eaten at lunchtime. In the afternoon it may perhaps be followed by singing or dancing in a town square, or on some islands a priest will process with an icon from house to house to confer blessings on each family.

There are some gorgeous photo books of Greece. These are my favorites: *Greece from the Air* by photographer Yann Arthus-Bertrand, a large-format collection of landscapes; *The Most Beautiful Villages of Greece* by Mark Ottaway with photos by Hugh Palmer; and *Timeless Places: Greek Isles* by Laura Brooks. *Greece: Land of Light* by Nicholas Gage with photos by Barry Brukoff has beautiful photos of the architecture and people as well as of the countryside.

*B*ooks

For your reading pleasure, I recommend the following:

During the 1930s, naturalist Gerald Durrell spend five years as a lad on the island of Corfu, and from this adventure came his book, *My Family and Other Animals.* Intensely interested in natural history at an early age, he describes his time spent there—the capers of his eccentric family of British expatriates, the creatures he constantly collects and studies, the Greek people who befriend him—all written in a breezy and amusing way.

One of the family members who plays a part in Durrell's story is his literary older brother Larry, better known to readers as Lawrence Durrell, famous for writing *The Alexandria*

Quartet. Lawrence also penned two memoirs about his time in Greece, and the better of them is *Prospero's Cell: A Guide to the Landscape and Manners of the Island of Corcyra.* It too is written about Corfu during a carefree time, the glory days before World War II. He describes the radiant landscape, the peasants and their customs, the fishermen, and his wonderful circle of wild and witty friends. A loving portrait of a different time.

The daughter of Greek immigrants to Australia, Katherine Kizilos is inspired by her dad's stories to travel to Greece and find her roots. She travels widely, visiting cities, islands, border zones, and finally her family's village in the mountains. Her book *The Olive Grove: Travels in Greece* not only describes the people and landscapes she encounters, but particularly explores national identity, and the changes that "progress" has brought to the traditional Greek way of life.

Patricia Storace, an American poet, wrote *Dinner with Persephone* about her experiences during a year spent in Greece. With lush prose she describes it, skillfully weaving in snippets of history and myth. The tension between past and present, Greek nationalism, the minutiae of her life, the landscape, her interactions with the locals all are described with sparkling wit. A fascinating portrait of contemporary Greece.

What better to read out loud than poetry? An excellent compilation entitled *Modern Greek Poetry* contains the work of thirty-two Greek poets of the nineteenth and twentieth centuries. It includes the poems of two Nobel Prize-winners, and is superbly translated by Kimon Friar.

Or you could tackle the Greek classics this weekend. The most appropriate of the epic poems would be Homer's *Odyssey*, about Odysseus' interminable voyage home to his beloved Ithaka. Having spent ten years fighting the Trojan wars, all he wants to do is get himself and his men safely home, but so many obstacles are thrown in his path that the journey takes another ten long hard years. Translations of this great work abound, not all of them good. In 1996 a new translation by award-winning translator Robert Fagles was published, and it has been widely acclaimed as beautifully poetic yet clear and accessible. I'd start there.

If it's a novel you are craving, you can't do better than *Zorba the Greek* by Nikos Kazantzakis, Greece's preeminent twentieth-century author. Set just prior World War I, it is the story of Basil, an introspective young Englishman who travels to Crete to manage a mine he has inherited. Along the way he meets Alexis Zorba, and is persuaded to offer him a job. The two are complete opposites. Basil lives his life cautiously, ruled by convention and logic, whereas the older Zorba is a sensualist who lives life to the fullest, embracing it with passion and exuberance. A friendship between these two gradually develops, and

Basil comes to realize that his ordered life is a lonely one, and that he has sacrificed the possibility of joy to the altar of control. It is beautifully written, and gives a fascinating portrait of life in a small Greek village at that time.

Another engrossing read is to be found in *Corelli's Mandolin,* written by Louis De Bernieres. This is a sweeping novel that covers fifty years in the lives of the people of the island of Cephallonia, from the 1940s to the present. With acerbic wit the author introduces us to the doctor and his beautiful daughter, her beloved fisherman, the villagers, and we follow them as Greece is invaded by Italy and Nazi Germany, and beyond. De Bernieres weaves it all in—romance, the horrors of war, political satire, history—brilliantly captured with intelligence and humor. (And if reading this book arouses your curiosity about its locale, a photo book devoted to bringing it alive for us, *Captain Corelli's Island: Cephallonia* by Terry and Andy Harris, has recently been published.)

The most intense work of modern fiction ever situated on a Greek isle is *The Magus* by John Fowles. In it, young Englishman Nicholas Urfe, fleeing a romantic entanglement, accepts a teaching position on the island of Phraxos.

There he is befriended by a wealthy owner of a palatial estate who derives his amusement from staging masques. Nicholas becomes involved, and the masques become increasingly elaborate and Byzantine. He finds himself barely able to discern between fact and fantasy, and struggles to hold on to reality. This book is eerie, complex, and eminently worth reading.

Movies

Never on Sunday (1960) is a lighthearted story of Piraeus' most popular prostitute, Ilya, played with vivacity by Melina Mercouri. She lives a life she loves, filled with lovers and music and laughter, until she meets a sensible Connecticut philosopher who thinks that she will be happier if he helps her to replace vice with culture. The reformation does not go quite as he plans. Great soundtrack, lots of fun.

Iphigenia (1977) is a powerfully moving Greek tragedy based on the play by Euripides. It's set immediately prior to the Trojan War, as the Greek Army, becalmed, waits impatiently for the change in weather that will allow them to launch their ships. Their leader makes a mistake that angers the gods, and in response an oracle offers him a terrible ultimatum. Irene

Papas as Clytemnestra and Tatiana Papamoschou as Iphigenia turn in bravura performances. You won't be able to find this at every video store, but it's worth calling around for.

Pauline Collins plays a fortysomething Liverpool housewife who's seriously stuck in a rut in *Shirley Valentine* (1989). Fate intervenes, and she flies off to the Greek Isles for an unexpected holiday, reconnecting with her younger, more carefree self while she's there. This starts off a bit slowly but it's well worth persevering because it has some very funny moments, and lovely scenery of Mykonos.

Mediterraneo (1991) is an absolutely delightful movie about a small band of Italian soldiers stationed on a quiet Greek island during World War II. Initially the island appears deserted, but everything is not as it seems, and soon the quirky band of Italians find that there could be worse places to wait out a war. An engaging cast, and shots of beautiful clear blue Aegean Sea.

And of course there is the perennial favorite, *Zorba the Greek* (1964). Filmed on the island of Corfu, it stars Anthony Quinn as the robust, exuberant Zorba the Greek, and Alan Bates as Basil, the conservative Englishman. Sometimes funny, sometimes dark, it won three Academy Awards and is well worth watching.

𝓜usic ·

If you are looking for folk music, *Greek Folk Favorites* by Panegyris is a compilation of traditional songs and dances, performed with great passion. The group features Dora Stratou, a maven in the Greek traditional music and dance world.

Once known as the music of the lower classes, *rembetika* (from the Turkish *rembet* meaning "from the gutter") is now popular with the hip crowd. Similar in spirit, though not in sound, to American urban blues, this musical style was born in the 1920s when Greece's unsuccessful invasion of Turkey led to 2 million refugees pouring out of Asia Minor into Greece. These people found themselves unwanted in a land that could barely support them, living a life of poverty and rejection. From their misery rembetika was born, sad songs that told of their struggles. *Mourmourike: Songs of the Greek Underworld,* consisting of recordings by various artists made between the 1930s and 1950s, gives a good introduction to the rembetiko form. With spirited performances of these songs from the darker side of Greek life, the CD also includes a fascinating booklet with lyric translations and an explanation of their context.

George Dalaras is often called "the Greek Bruce Spring-steen," and few performers there are so well loved. He's made dozens of albums; for an introduction to his powerful voice and rembetika-inspired pop music, I recommend his 1998 release *A Portrait.*

Another artist who blends pop with traditional music is Haris Alexiou. Tremendously popular in Greece for her deep, powerful voice, she's been recording since the 1970s, but only recently has she had her first U.S. release, *Di Efchen.* It's well worth a listen.

Athenian singer Savina Yannatou has a wonderful, haunting voice—think Enya goes Greek. Her album *Mediterranea: Songs of the Mediterranean* includes songs from over a dozen of the countries that border the Mediterranean. Though it's not solely Greek, her voice is so lovely that you won't mind.

Although he's most famous in North America as the com-poser of the film score for *Zorba the Greek,* Mikis Theodorakis justly deserves the title of Greece's greatest composer. He's written symphonies, operas, and ballets, as well as a large body of popular music in the traditional style—there seems to be nothing musical to which he cannot turn his hand. There's an absolute wealth of recorded material available, but I recom-mend *The Very Best of Mikis Theodorakis,* an all-instrumental album that showcases his wide range of musical styles.

If you're on the musically adventurous side, more into clubs than the folk dance scene, you may enjoy *Greek Fire* by Annabouboula. They're a trio of New York Greeks who play a terrific blend of traditional instrumentation on songs that would not be out of place at a rave.

Food

Greek cooking is best known for simple preparation and clear, strong flavors. Lots of tomatoes, herbs, and of course good-quality olive oil. Here are some excellent Greek cookbooks, although they are by no means the only ones:

The Foods of the Greek Islands: Cooking and Culture at the Crossroads of the Mediterranean by Aglaia Kremezi. The author, who won a Julia Child Award for her previous book *The Foods of Greece,* traveled the islands extensively to collect recipes from locals. There are island-by-island food profiles, and a wealth of fresh, simple, but delicious recipes. As you'd expect, seafood features prominently. Illustrated with color photography.

The Complete Book of Greek Cooking by the Recipe Club of Saint Paul's Greek Orthodox Church is a perennial favorite. This book was first published in the 1960s as a fund raiser for the church in Hempstead, New York, and also as a way to preserve recipes that people had learned at their mothers' knees. It's been updated and improved more than once, and is still going strong. The food is authentically Greek, and the easy-to-follow recipes were written by everyday cooks. Also has good how-to information on topics such as working with phyllo dough.

In their review of *The Food and Wine of Greece* by Diane Kochilas, the *Washington Post* said, "There has never been a better, more comprehensive book on Greek cuisine." Quite a recommendation! This book covers lots more than just the classic dishes. The author has also written the excellent and innovative *Greek Vegetarian: More Than 100 Recipes Inspired by the Traditional Dishes and Flavors of Greece,* which includes such dishes as Green Bean Ragout with Mint and Sun-Dried Tomatoes, and Villager's Leek and Fennel Pie.

Greek Cuisine by Vefa Alexiadou—this woman in serious! Renowned as the leading cooking authority in Greece, Vefa Alexiadou regularly teaches cooking on Greek television, and is on the board of the Center for the Preservation and Advancement of Traditional Greek Gastronomy. Her goal with this and all her books is to pass on the heritage and authentic flavor of traditional Greek cookery while updating recipes to use modern methods and equipment.

For your Greek weekend, I'm suggesting a very traditional but delicious Greek meal: avogolemono soup, lamb kebobs, and baklava. Fill in with rice and a salad of cucumbers, tomatoes, feta cheese, and Kalamata olives dressed with olive oil and red wine vinegar, and you'll be all set!

For another evening, you could also go a completely different route and make a terrific meal entirely of appetizers. If you and your weekend companions are not in the mood for working with phyllo dough or rolling grape leaves, almost all of these dishes can be found in the take-out section of specialty grocery stores, or could be ordered to go from your local Greek restaurant: olives; chunks of feta cheese; *spanakopita* (phyllo triangles with spinach); *tryopites* (phyllo triangles with cheese); *dolmas* (stuffed grape leaves); hummus (chick pea and tahini dip) with pita bread; tzatziki (herbed yogurt and cucumber); *keftedakia marinata* (marinated spiced meatballs); *marides marinates* (marinated smelts).

Make Mine Red

Although Greece is not known for making the absolute finest wines, it does make some that are well within the realm of acceptable. So what the heck, go for a Greek wine with dinner. *Wine Spectator* considers that four deserve their Good rating. All are from the Boutari Winery, and the 1997 Nemea is the best value for money: 1996 Merlot-Xinomavro Vin de Pays d'Imathia; 1997 Nemea; 1996 Agiorgitiko Nemea; 1998 Santorini.

Avogolemono Soup

There are dozens of versions of this classic Greek soup.

5 cups chicken stock	1 teaspoon lemon zest
7 tablespoons long-grain white rice	coarse salt, to taste
3 eggs	freshly ground black pepper, to taste
juice of 2 lemons	chopped fresh dill, for garnish

Bring the stock to a boil in a medium saucepan. Gradually add the rice, stirring constantly. Reduce heat, cover, and simmer until rice is tender, about 9–12 minutes.

Meanwhile, beat the eggs, lemon juice, and lemon zest together in a large bowl. When the rice is cooked, slowly pour in a very thin stream half of the hot broth into the eggs to temper them, whisking constantly. Then slowly whisk the egg yolk mixture into the broth and place over low heat.

Cook, stirring constantly and without allowing soup to boil, just long enough to thicken. Season to taste with salt and pepper, and garnish serving bowls with chopped dill. Serves 4.

A Walk on the Wild Side . . .

Get a bottle of retsina, the piney-flavored traditional wine. Retsina goes back to Homer's day, when to prevent spoilage, clay amphorae of wine were sealed with resin. Some say it tastes like turpentine, others like it—why don't you judge for yourself? Chilling heightens the resin flavor, so be sure to serve it at room temperature, preferably as they'd do it in Greece, in tumblers. Here are a couple of recommended brands: Achaia Clauss nonvintage Retsina Appellation Traditionelle; Gaia Vineyards Ritinitis Nobilis.

Lamb Kebabs

1 3½ lb. leg of lamb, cut into
    1½-inch chunks
¼ cup olive oil
¼ cup red wine
juice of 1½ lemons
2 tablespoons dried oregano, preferably
    Greek, or 4 tablespoons chopped fresh
1 tablespoon dried rosemary, or
    2 tablespoons chopped fresh

4 garlic cloves, chopped
½ teaspoon salt
¼ teaspoon freshly ground black pepper
1 large onion, cut into 1-inch pieces
1 red or green bell pepper, cut into
    1-inch pieces
½ basket cherry tomatoes

Place the lamb in a glass or ceramic bowl. Mix the next eight ingredients together and pour over the lamb. Cover and marinate in the refrigerator, preferably overnight, or for at least 3 hours, turning the meat from time to time.

Remove lamb and reserve marinade. Thread the lamb onto long metal skewers, alternating with the chunks of onions, peppers, and the cherry tomatoes. Grill over hot coals, turning frequently and brushing with the remaining marinade. Serves 4.

Baklava

Baklava is a special occasion dish. If you have never made it, don't be apprehensive; it's a little fiddly working with the phyllo, but is otherwise foolproof. The word *baklava* comes from the Farsi meaning "many leaves."

Syrup

1 cup honey	rind of 1 lemon
2 cups sugar	1 stick cinnamon
1½ cups water	4 whole cloves
2 tablespoons lemon juice	¼ teaspoon ground cardamom

Filling

1 lb. walnuts or blanched almonds, finely chopped (about 4 cups)	1 teaspoon ground cinnamon
¼ cup sugar	¼ teaspoon ground cloves
	¼ teaspoon ground cardamom

Dough

1 lb. (about 24 sheets) phyllo dough
about 1 cup (2 sticks) melted sweet butter

Combine all of the syrup ingredients in a saucepan and bring to a boil, stirring occasionally. Lower the heat and simmer for 10 minutes. Remove and discard the lemon rind, cinnamon sticks, and whole cloves, then let syrup cool.

While syrup is cooling, combine the filling ingredients.

Preheat the oven to 350°F. Grease a 12-by-9-inch or 13-by-9-inch baking pan. Take phyllo dough from container, spread flat, and cover with a damp towel. Replace towel over the dough after every time you remove a sheet, to prevent it drying out. Place a sheet of phyllo in the prepared pan and lightly brush with melted butter. Repeat with 8 more sheets, buttering each one. Spread with half of the filling. Top with 8 more sheets, brushing each with butter. Use any torn sheets in the middle layer. Spread with the remaining nut mixture and end with a top layer of 8 sheets, continuing to brush each with butter. Trim any overhanging edges.

Using a long, sharp knife, cut six equal lengthwise strips (about $1^3/_4$ inches wide) through the pastry. Make $1^1/_2$-inch-wide diagonal cuts across the strips to form diamond shapes. Just before baking, lightly sprinkle the top of the pastry with cold water to inhibit the pastry from curling. Bake for 20 minutes. Reduce the heat to 300°F and bake about 25 additional minutes, until golden brown.

Drizzle the syrup slowly over the hot baklava then let it stand for about 2 hours. Makes about 36 small diamond-shaped pastries.

—Jenny Collins

The Magic of Morocco

MOROCCO is a land of exotic appeal. Travelers have gone there for centuries to experience its powerful mystique. The blending of Islamic, Berber, African, and European cultures creates an unforgettable experience. Upon arrival, the sights, sounds, and smells of this land of sea, sand, and snow assail your senses. The bustling *souks* (markets), such as the Place Djemaael-Fna in Marrakech, host jugglers, storytellers, snake charmers, open-air food stalls, and vendors selling prized Moroccan carpets, woodwork, jewelry, and leather. The strong smells of spices, mint, saffron, turmeric, cumin, and cinnamon waft through the air. Around you people are conversing in Moroccan

Setting the Scene

Arabic, French, Spanish, English, or one of the three distinct Berber languages. The vibrant orange, reds, and yellows of the carpets in the souks are juxtaposed against the azure sky and the dark blue cotton worn by the nomads.

It's not difficult to experience the magic of Morocco in your own home. First, move all the furniture against the walls, and bring out rugs and large pillows to lounge on—the more colorful the better. While the exterior of many Moroccan homes is sedate (usually brown or white), inside the many rugs and pillows are brightly colored in deep red, oranges, and yellows.

If you wish to decorate yourself as well, consider henna. Applying henna designs to your hands and feet is a popular tradition throughout the Middle East, Africa, and in certain parts of Asia. Traditionally used for brides on their wedding day, henna has recently become quite popular in the West. For your Moroccan getaway, you can create henna designs for yourself, your family, or guests that will last four to six weeks. Green henna powder is mixed with water, and sometimes lemon juice or tea, to create a paste that will dye your skin red. Henna kits, powder, and the intricate designs can be found in many beauty outlets.

No matter what you decide to do on this adventure, begin by serving Moroccan mint tea, sweetened with sugar. Tea, a very large part of Moroccan culture today, was introduced by the British in the mid-nineteenth century. Unlike the British custom, there is no specific tea time. Throughout the cities and villages, you will find numerous cafés serving tea, and tea will always be offered to you when visiting homes, before and after meals, or even by eager vendors in the souks. After brewing your own version of this Moroccan classic, sit back, relax and begin your journey through this exotic land.

Tea, Morocco-style

To make proper Moroccan tea, first rinse your teapot with boiling water, then take black tea or Chinese green tea and add boiling water to it. Add a handful of fresh mint, sugar to taste, and let the mixture steep for 3–4 minutes. Once the tea is ready, pour into tiny glasses, add a sprig of mint, and serve.

The proper tea ceremony has the host or hostess bring out the teapot on a tray surrounded by tiny boxes containing the mint, sugar, and tea. After combining the ingredients and letting them steep, the host proceeds to pour the tea from a great height into one glass. The first glass is always examined, and then poured back into the pot. Then, the rest of the glasses are filled.

Books

To further set the mood for your Moroccan getaway, take a look at these beautiful photographic books:

Morocco: Sahara to the Sea by Mary Cross begins with a preface by the famous expatriate Paul Bowles and an introduction by the Moroccan writer Tahar Ben Jalloun. This is a visually stunning collection of photographs of the people and places of Morocco—from the Sahara Desert in the south to the Rif Mountains in the north—depicting life in both the large cities and small villages. The haunting landscapes, beautiful architecture, and people of the various regions all provide a great pictorial overview of this diverse country.

Morocco Modern by Herbert J. M. Ypma is a collection of beautiful photos depicting the architecture and artistry of Moroccan buildings and homes. Rich with color, the photos offer a wide variety of decorative objects and architectural spaces that combine the best historical artistry of Morocco's past with the modern Islamic nation Morocco is today.

Maroc by Albert Watson is a collection of black-and-white photos combined with Arabic calligraphy that really creates the feeling of Morocco—both its past and present.

Beware if you choose Fodor's *Escape to Morocco* by Pamela Windo. You will be packing your bags and taking the first flight to Marrakech! This is a unique combination of a photographic travel book, guide, and commentary on each of the regions in Morocco. Windo takes you from the Mediterranean coast to the blue villages of the Rif Mountains. You explore the Roman ruins in Fez, the markets in Marrakech, the snowy peaks in the Atlas Mountains, and even take a trip to watch the sun set over the Sahara Desert.

If you are looking for something meatier, there are many novels that describe the sociopolitical aspects of the country, especially the lives of women in an Islamic country. In *Dreams of Trespass,* Fatimi Mernissi weaves fantasy and memory together as she presents life in 1940s Fez from a ten-year-old girl's perspective at a time when harem life was still an acceptable part of society.

Another famous Moroccan writer, Tahar Ben Jalloun, has written two books that critique Arab social customs and Islamic law. Starting with *The Sand Child* and concluding with *The Sacred Night,* these two novels tell the story of Mohammed Ahmed, a Moroccan girl being raised as a boy by her father to overcome the Islamic laws of inheritance.

An expatriate in Morocco for forty years, Paul Bowles wrote the 1949 classic, *The Sheltering Sky.* In it, the Sahara Desert is just as much a character and protagonist as the three Americans, Kit, Tunner, and Port. The psychological terror in *The Sheltering Sky* is not for the faint-hearted, but it is a fascinating examination of how these three travelers deal (or rather not deal) with the alien culture of North Africa. Bernardo Bertolucci adapted the novel into a film in 1990 starring Debra Winger and John Malkovich. While the film provides gorgeous scenery of Morocco, I would definitely recommend the book over the movie.

Hideous Kinky by Esther Freud is another tale told from the perspective of a child. Set in the 1960s, a hippie mother takes her two young girls, Bea and Lucy, to Morocco in search of spirituality. In the beginning, the exotic appeal of the culture and customs of the land fascinate the two girls. As the novel progresses, however, they yearn for the comforts of home. A poignant tale, it was made into a movie in 1998, starring Kate Winslet. I loved this book, and the movie is a good adaptation of Freud's novel.

*V*ideos

Of course no getaway weekend to Morocco would be complete without watching *Casablanca.* Although this classic 1942 film is not "authentically" Moroccan (it was filmed in California), *Casablanca* helped start a fascination with Morocco. This quintessential romantic movie, depicting the longing, passion, and sometimes difficult choices we are sometimes forced to make, *Casablanca* tells the story of Rick (Humphrey Bogart), an exiled American, and Ilsa (Ingrid Bergman), his lost love from Paris. The movie went on to win an Academy Award for Best Picture in 1944, and the famous parting line, "Here's looking at you, kid," will force even the most stalwart to shed a tear or two.

Filmed in 1930, *Morocco* with Marlene Dietrich and Gary Cooper is another recommended "classic" for a Moroccan movie marathon. Dietrich plays a cabaret singer stuck in Morocco when the Foreign Legion arrives.

Moroccan Movie-Making

Hollywood loves using Morocco for location shoots depicting many different time periods and most Middle Eastern countries. Here is a surprising list of favorite movies and television programs shot in Morocco: *The Mummy* (1999), *The Mummy Returns* (2001), *Gladiator* (2000), *Arabian Nights* (1999), *Cleopatra* (1999), *The Last Temptation of Christ* (1988), *Jewel of the Nile* (1985), *Spies Like Us* (1985).

Another perennial, *Lawrence of Arabia* with Peter O'Toole provides a fascinating look at life in the Sahara among the Bedouin tribes. Although the story focuses on the history of Saudi Arabia, it does begin in Morocco where the young T. E. Lawrence is stationed during World War I. Filmed in 1962, it went on to win seven Academy Awards.

Music

Like the country itself, Moroccan music is an eclectic mix of musical traditions—the classical style from the Andulusian heritage in Spain, the storytelling traditions of the Berbers, and the contemporary fusion of African and French pop and rock. Here are a few of the best:

Gharnati: Arabo-Andulusian Music of Morocco by Amina Alaoui is a soft, bedtime classic. A favorite Moroccan artist, Amina's soft haunting voice will take you back through the centuries.

Sabil' A Salaam by Nass Marrakech takes the Gnawa tradition of trance music and combines it with Indian and West African percussion and Japanese flutes—a great collection for a mellow gathering of friends.

If you want music that will make you want to dance try *Berber: Music from the High Atlas Mountains* by various artists. This joyous music is often heard at weddings or during other ceremonial occasions.

A Moroccan friend recommended *Jilala: Sufi Trance Music From Morocco*. I fell in love with it immediately. This is a collection of music by the Sufi mystical sect of Jilala originally recorded by Paul Bowles and Brion Gysin in 1965.

Food

As with Moroccan music, Moroccan food represents the rich cultural heritage of the land. Sharing meals is central to Moroccan way of life. By emphasizing strong family and tribal traditions, food is used to celebrate every aspect of life.

The typical Moroccan meal is served family-style and eaten with your hands. In the middle of the room, place a large tablecloth. Around it put the pillows to lean against. The main dish could be a *couscous* or *tajine* (a meat dish with two vegetables). Surrounding the main dish, smaller plates of cooked and raw salads are served: olives, cooked eggplant and tomatoes, cucumbers and green peppers in a vinaigrette, carrot and orange salad. Bread is a staple at every meal. In Morocco, bread is made in the morning and then taken to one of the communal wood-fired ovens to be baked. Amazingly, the bakers know which loaves of bread go to which family just by looking at the dough.

If you decide to eat with your hands, begin by serving small bowls of flower-scented water to wash hands in. After the meal is served, return again with fresh water and towels so diners can clean up after the feast. At the end of the meal, dessert is served, which almost always is a variety of fruit. And, of course

after all the food is cleared away, the mint tea is brought out again—with the mint acting as an excellent digestive. Now you can relax, talk, listen to music, and, for the truly adventurous, offer a belly dance performance. Although belly dancing is not specifically Moroccan, belly dancers are hired for special occasions and weddings.

For one meal, I have chosen couscous with lemon chicken and olives; orange, date and almond

Spirited Choices

It is against Islamic tradition to consume alcohol. There are, however, some wines and beers that are produced in Morocco, and non-Muslims can purchase alcohol at most bars and restaurants in the cities. If you are not a teetotaler, for your Moroccan weekend check out specialty wine and beer stores to try Flag, Stork, and, yes, Casablanca beer. If you prefer wine, there are the Gueroune Reds, made at the foot of the Atlas Mountains, or Ksar (which means "palace"), a nice white wine.

salad; Moroccan carrot salad; and a bell pepper and tomato salad. Serve this meal with bread and finish it off with a selection of fruits, and don't forget the mint tea!

In addition to the recipes offered here, there are several good cookbooks that offer a range of Moroccan delights. My favorites are Paula Woffert's *Couscous and Other Good Food from Morocco,* Madhur Jaffrey's *World Vegetarian,* which contains many wonderful vegetarian recipes of Morocco, *Cooking at the Kasbah: Recipes from My Moroccan Kitchen* by Kitty Morse and *Café Morocco* by Anissa Helou.

Couscous with Lemon, Chicken and Olives

While traditionally couscous is made from scratch, today in most Moroccan homes, as in the United States, store-bought varieties are used. Making couscous is a very labor-intensive process, but if you would like to read more, check out Paula Woffert's *Couscous and Other Good Food from Morocco.*

1 medium onion, peeled	¼ teaspoon saffron threads
1 garlic clove, peeled	¼ teaspoon salt
4 boneless, skinless chicken breasts	3 tablespoons lemon juice
2 tablespoons flour	grated peel of 2 lemons
1 tablespoon olive oil	½ cup green olives, pitted and chopped
1 cup water	2 tablespoon minced cilantro
½ teaspoon ground ginger	fresh ground black pepper, to taste
½ teaspoon ground cumin	1 cup couscous
½ teaspoon paprika	

Quarter the onion and chop it coarsely together with the garlic in a food processor. Coat both sides of the chicken breasts with flour. In a large skillet, heat the olive oil over medium heat, add the garlic-onion mixture and the chicken and sauté until golden, about 10 minutes.

Stir in 1 cup water and add the ginger, cumin, paprika, saffron, salt, half the lemon juice, and lemon peel. Bring this mixture to a boil, reduce heat, and simmer, covered, for 35 minutes.

Remove the chicken breasts from the sauce and allow them to cool a few minutes. Cut the chicken into small pieces and put them back into the sauce, adding in the remaining lemon juice, olives, cilantro, and pepper. Simmer gently for 5 minutes.

While the chicken is cooking, make the couscous according to the directions on the package. Spoon chicken mixture over couscous and serve. Serves 4.

Orange, Date and Almond Salad

1 head romaine lettuce	$\frac{1}{2}$ teaspoon ground cinnamon, plus
3 navel or temple oranges	more to taste
2 tablespoons lemon juice	1 tablespoon orange flower water
2 tablespoons sugar	$\frac{1}{3}$ cup almonds, chopped
salt to taste	$\frac{1}{3}$ cup dates, chopped

Wash the lettuce, cutting it into bite-size pieces, storing in the refrigerator until needed.

Peel the oranges and remove all the outside membranes and seeds. Then section the oranges by cutting away all the membranes from the orange flesh. Place in a small mixing bowl, squeezing the juice from the remainder of the orange over the sections. Cover and store in the refrigerator until needed.

To make the dressing, mix the lemon juice, sugar, salt, $\frac{1}{2}$ teaspoon cinnamon, and orange flower water. Just before serving, toss the lettuce and oranges with the dressing. Place the salad on individual plates and garnish with the almonds and dates, adding a dash of cinnamon. Serves 4.

Carrot Salad

1 lb. carrots	2 tablespoons olive oil
1 teaspoon salt	1 clove garlic, minced
1 teaspoon ground cumin	juice of 1 lemon
1 teaspoon paprika	1 tablespoon parsley
1/4 teaspoon white pepper	

Peel and cut the carrots into 1/4-inch slices. In a saucepan, bring water to boil, adding the carrots and salt. Cook the carrots until tender but still with some bite. Drain and cool.

Mix together the cumin, paprika, white pepper, olive oil, minced garlic, lemon juice, and parsley. Toss with the carrots and refrigerate. Serve at room temperature. Serves 4.

Bell Pepper and Tomato Salad

You can buy roasted peppers to make this dish, which really cuts down on the preparation time.

3 large red bell peppers	ground pepper to taste
3 medium, ripe tomatoes, peeled and seeded	1/2 teaspoon sugar
	1 clove garlic, crushed
1 tablespoon red wine vinegar	1/4 cup olive oil

Grill the red peppers by cutting them in half, seeding and broiling cut-side down until skin blisters and blackens. Peel off the skin and cut into 3/4-inch pieces. Cut the tomatoes into 3/4-inch pieces and mix together with the peppers.

Combine vinegar, pepper, sugar, garlic, and olive oil. Stir into pepper-tomato mixture and marinate for 10 minutes before serving. Serves 4.

—Heather McArthur

Into Africa

A WEEKEND trip to East Africa is an adventure into the very visceral roots of our species and offers one of the world's most visually stunning displays. It starts when you get off the airplane and cannot believe how brilliantly deep blue the sky is, and then it never lets up. Stunning savannas, a lake covered with swarming pink flamingos, tropical jungles teeming with so much life that the expansive canopy itself seems to breath and chatter, violent lightning storms across the expanse of Lake Victoria, Mt. Kilimanjaro poking its snow-tipped peak towering over some of the most extraordinary game reserves in

Setting the Scene

Africa. East Africa is a location everyone should see at least once in their life.

Technically, East Africa includes the old colonial states of Kenya, Uganda, Tanganyika, Rwanda, Burundi, and most of Zanzibar, and is certainly one of the more diverse regions of the world both in terms of peoples and ecology. Among the better known people to populate East Africa were our first ancestors (including *Australopithecus africanus* and *robustus*), the Twa Pygmies, the Nomadic Watutsi and Maasai, Arab Muslims who arrived from Persia during the eighth century, and an assortment of Europeans from the Portuguese, British, and Germans to the Belgians intent on profiting from the bountiful resources of this land. The land itself includes the largest (by area) lake in the world (Lake Victoria), impressive mountain peaks, and more game reserves and wildlife than anywhere else on the continent.

Ironically, the game reserves that form much of the attraction for tourists to the area are also the case of some of East Africa's most pressing and thorny problems—the ongoing competition between the burgeoning population of people and the decidedly undomesticated animal life. It's difficult to farm when elephants have a tendency to wander through your fields; difficult for the pastoral tribes to graze their cattle when they are ever in danger of being caught and punished for trespassing in a game reserve; and in the meantime the tourist buses careening at will through parks are creating their own devastation.

To do East Africa properly, you should pick a hot summer weekend to capture the mood. One thematic option is to make sure everyone is appropriately dressed in khakis, cotton or linen short-sleeve shirts, and safari hats if you can muster them up. Decorate your home in full safari, with lions, elephants, black rhino, leopards, zebras, giraffes, and warthogs aplenty. With a bit of digging at your local poster outlets you can usually find a large poster or two of assorted African wildlife with the east African savanna shimmering in the background or maybe posters of the gorillas in the mist of Rwanda to hang on walls. If that doesn't work, try raiding a second hand children's toy store and pick up some wildlife picture books, or, in a pinch, scatter a few stuffed animals around.

Another possible theme you could organize around is the "Dawn of Humans." As far as archeologists have been able to determine, our species emerged somewhere in the Rift Valley, either in Olduvai Gorge in what is now Tanzania or around Lake Turkana in modern Kenya. As the "cradle of humanity," East Africa has one of the greatest diversity of languages, representing virtually every modern African language spoken.

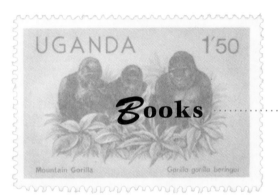

Books

To further the nature ambience, there are a few photo books worth considering. For an unparalleled experience of the visceral feel of the East African savanna and wildlife, get *Serengeti: Natural Order on the African Plain* by Mitsuaki Iwago. It is absolutely stunning!

For a view into the fascinating and colorful riches of the East African culture, select from one of a handful of beautiful photo books by Angela Fisher and Carol Beckwith. Both together and separately, these two photographers have produced a body of work broad and diverse enough to engender a bit of controversy. Both photographers are trying to capture some of the stunningly beautiful and unique images of what is in fact a

Endangered Species

One of the more pressing problems in East Africa is the increasing plight of many of the Earth's more spectacular species. The dwindling population of gorillas has been well documented but is still of deep concern. Perhaps the most threatened of the big game animals is the black rhino. With an undeserved reputation as a fearsome animal, it has been a long favorite of big-game hunters, but it is commerce, not wild-eyed hunters, which is threatening to drive the rhino into extinction. From a population of more than 20,000 thirty years ago, the black rhino in East Africa now number fewer than 500. In a slaughter reminiscent of the destruction of the North American buffalo, the rhino are tracked down by sophisticated poachers to get the horn, which is prized in Chinese medicine and as the ultimate dagger handle in parts of the Mideast. Rhino horn is currently selling for over $10,000 a pound on the black market.

A number of years back the elephant population was headed in the same direction due to the demand for ivory. Fortunately the international community responded in time with a well-enforced ban on the exporting of ivory from Africa. That ban had the desired effect, and elephant populations have rebounded well (some neighbors might claim too well) in most of East Africa.

disappearing culture and have been criticized by those who feel that their work is more staged and nostalgic than an accurate reflection of today's Africa. That might be true, but it takes nothing away from the quality, texture, beauty, and representative nature of their work. Among their best in my opinion are *Maasai* by Tepilit Ole Saitoti and Carol Beckwith, *African Ceremonies* by Carol Beckwith and Angela Fisher, and *Africa Adorned* by Angela Fisher.

In a more literary vein, if you really want to dive into the African experience and at the same time read a book that will stick with you for the rest of your life, I recommend starting with Chinua Achebe's *Things Fall Apart* (1958). Achebe is Nigerian, but this book is every bit as relevant to the modern East African experience. *Things Fall Apart* is the book that launched the modern African novel. It is important not only for its historic value, but for the simple power of its prose, which has come to characterize the best of African writing.

Weep Not Child by Ngugi wa Thiong'o is often considered the East African equivalent of *Things Fall Apart,* and it was the first novel in English out of Kenya. *Weep Not Child* can be difficult to find but is worth the effort. If you can't find a copy, look for *Devil on the Cross* (1989), also by Ngugi wa Thiong'o, which is wonderfully funny, quirky, powerful, and tragic. Ngugi wrote

Devil on the Cross in Gikuyu (his native language) and then translated it himself into English.

A powerful book that captures the modern African experience with a textual depth that is almost chilling was written by an Indian. *A Bend in the River* by V. S. Naipaul is a view of East Africa from the perennial outsider. Naipaul, one of the world's literary giants, is literally a man without a country, and in *A Bend in the River,* he turned his extraordinary powers of perception and description on the struggles of people in postcolonial Africa. A must book for any cosmopolitan traveler/reader.

The Birthplace of Humanity

Recent DNA research by Swedish scientists place our first ancestors in the Rift Valley approximately 150,000 years ago. The migration out of Africa began approximately 30,000 years ago—a brief blink of the eye in geological terms—as humans headed north to the Middle East and from there east, colonizing southern and southeast Asia as well as China. A part of that eastward migration kept right on going down through the Indonesian archipelago and on to Australia, while another branch headed north across the Bering Strait into Alaska. The very last areas to be "colonized" were Europe and North and South America.

Videos

For the pure backdrop experience of East Africa, you can't do better than *National Geographic's Africa Animal Oasis* (1992). Filmed in the breathtaking Ngorongoro Crater, which packs more animal life into a more concentrated area than anywhere else in the world, this hour-long video is the ultimate story of the daily fight to survive.

If you want the backdrop with a bit more Hollywood presentation, you can't go wrong with *Out of Africa* (1985), the Oscar-winning epic starring Meryl Streep and Robert Redford about writer Isak Dinesen's life. Beautifully photographed with a compelling love story, this one's sure to please.

For classic movie buffs, check out director John Ford's *Mogambo,* a 1953 remake of an even older classic (*Red Dust,* 1932). This entertaining film was shot on location in East Africa and has a powerful cast that includes Clark Gable, Ava Gardner, and Grace Kelly.

Still in the Hollywood vein are two strikingly different views (in all respects) of the same famous incident that took place in Kenya in 1898 and involved a man-eating lion that stalked the railroad workers around Kima. The first is *The Ghost and the Darkness,* a 1996 film staring Michael Douglas, which is a decent adventure/thriller with a touch of depth to it. On the other end of the spectrum is *Bwana Devil* (1952), one of the truly worst movies ever produced, so bad it is really worth watching. Unfortunately *Bwana Devil* was never released as a video, so if you want to see it you need to keep your eye on the late, late, late night movies. My favorite scenes involve a stuffed lion nailed to a long board being pushed and pulled backward and forward while actors scream in feigned terror. Another classic not in video but worth taping if you get the chance is the 1980 film *The Rise and Fall of Idi Amin.*

General African-related films worth watching are *The African Queen* (1951), the John Huston classic with Humphrey Bogart and Katharine Hepburn; *A Dry White Season* (1989) a gem of a film about South Africa in the days of apartheid; and the endearing *The Gods Must Be Crazy* (1980), which chronicles in all its innocence a Kalahari tribe's encounter with modern technology in the form of a Coke bottle.

Music

For mood music, you can get a copy of either *Into Africa,* one of the "Sounds of Earth" series, or *Jungle Talk: The Natural Sounds of the Wilderness,* a part of the "Echoes of Nature" series. Both are great background CDs with all the appropriate sounds you would hear if your tent was pitched somewhere on the plains of east Africa. *Jungle Talk* is more representative of the western portion of East Africa, around Rwanda, while *Into Africa* is the sound of the savanna, but for atmosphere either will do fine.

For a taste of modern East African music a compilation called *The Music of Kenya and Tanzania* or a couple of CDs called *Music From Uganda 1* and *Music From Uganda 2* do a great job of covering the range. For a fabulous collection of traditional music, pick up a copy of *Witchcraft & Ritual Music: Kenya & Tanzania.* Some of it is a bit chilling, but it is a beautiful collection.

Nyungu Chepuo
Ruttya frutios

Food

Coming up with a great menu for an East African weekend can be a bit of a challenge. While North African cuisine is understandably world famous, and West African cooking is beginning to be recognized, there really doesn't appear to be much depth to East Africa cuisine. The staple of every meal is a "mealie," which is a bean, sorghum, or maize paste that is rolled into a ball and dipped into assorted sauces, and the closest thing to a signature dish is barbecued goat.

My suggestion for an entrée would be a spicy meat stew with bean mealie, or if you wanted something lighter, the bean and fish stew with maize mealie. If the traditional fare sounds a bit daunting, you can try the "adapted" version of a continent classic, peanut stew. If the recipes following don't do it for you, I suggest getting *The Africa Cookbook,* which admittedly picks and chooses from the entire continent; it is not only a good cookbook but also a wonderful history of much of the development of African cuisine.

Spicy Meat Stew

1 lb. boneless pork	1 medium onion
1 teaspoon each cardamom and cumin	4 cloves garlic
1/2 teaspoon each black pepper and paprika	3 tablespoon oil
	3/4 cup coconut milk

Cut the pork into bite-sized strips. Combine the cardamom, cumin, black pepper, and paprika in a large bowl. Add the pork and toss to coat completely.

Chop the onion and garlic. In a large frying pan, heat the oil over medium-high heat and add the onion and garlic. Cook until the onion becomes translucent. Then add the pork strips and cook till browned. Add the coconut milk, cover, and simmer 20 minutes. Serves 4.

Bean Mealie

Traditionally mealie is rolled into balls by hand and dipped into the Spiced Meat Stew sauce. It takes a bit of practice, and you have to get the consistency just right to pull it off, so to be on the safe side you but could always use a spoon or fork to grab and dip.

1/2 cup white or navy beans	salt
1 onion	3 tablespoons peanut butter
2 tablespoon oil	water
3 teaspoon flour	

Cook the beans in plenty of water until tender (about 20 minutes). Drain.

Chop the onion and fry in oil over medium-high heat until translucent, about 10 minutes. Add flour and stir, constantly, till brown. Mash the beans and add them to the frying pan with the salt and peanut butter. Stir, adding water as needed to get a good stiff but pliable consistency. Form into balls around the size of a golf ball; dip each ball into the stew and eat. Serves 4.

Beans and Fish Stew

2 cups white or navy beans	2 tablespoon oil
water	1½ cups chopped tomatoes
2 onions	1 lb. fresh fish filets
4 cloves garlic	paprika or cayenne pepper to taste

Cover beans with plenty of water and cook till tender (about 20 minutes). Drain and reserve the water.

Chop the onions and garlic and fry in oil over medium-high heat until onions are translucent, about 10 minutes. Add the chopped tomatoes and simmer slowly for 10 minutes. Add the fish and enough water to cover the fish fully, and mix gently. Add either paprika or cayenne pepper to taste, then simmer until the fish is tender (about 10 minutes). Serves 4.

Maize Mealie

2 cups corn meal	2 tablespoons chopped fresh rosemary,
2 cups water	thyme, or oregano

Boil all ingredients until you have a smooth pliable mealie (about 15 minutes). Roll mealie into golf ball-sized balls and dip into the Bean and Fish Stew. Serves 4.

Grilled Corn on the Cob

This is one of the more common street dishes in Nairobi.

4 ears corn	2 tablespoons chopped fresh rosemary,
2 tablespoons butter	thyme, or oregano

Peel back the corn husks and remove as much of the silk as possible. Reserve the husks. Blend the butter and the fresh herb together, and rub mixture into the corn kernels. Replace the corn husks and grill, turning often, for approximately 10 minutes, or until corn is tender. Serves 4.

Curried Cabbage

This relatively common dish celebrates the long history of Indian influence in East Africa.

1 large onion	1½ cups canned, chopped tomatoes
1 large green or red bell pepper	2 tablespoons curry powder
2 tablespoons vegetable oil	water
½ small green cabbage, chopped	

Chop the onion and peppers. Heat the oil over medium-high heat and add the onions and peppers. Cook until soft, about 10 minutes. Add the cabbage, tomatoes, and curry, and simmer, covered, for 30 minutes. Add a bit of water if necessary to keep from sticking. Serves 4.

Peanut Stew

1³/₄ lb. boneless chicken, pork, or beef

3 tablespoons peanut oil

2 chopped onions

4 cloves chopped garlic

1 teaspoon curry power

¹/₂ teaspoon coriander

red pepper to taste

2¹/₂ cups chicken broth

2 medium chopped tomatoes

1 inch fresh ginger, minced

¹/₂ cup crunchy peanut butter

¹/₄ cup chopped, toasted peanuts

Chop the meat into bite-sized pieces; heat the oil in a large pot and brown the meat. Add the chopped onions and cook 5 minutes. Add the chopped garlic, curry, coriander, and red pepper, and stir to coat ingredients. Add the chicken broth, chopped tomatoes, and ginger. Cover and simmer for 40 minutes. Then add the peanut butter, stir, and cook uncovered for another 10 minutes. Serve over white rice and sprinkle the chopped peanuts on top.

— *Will Glennon*

A Musical Wonderland in St. Petersburg

WITH its wintry climate, more than sixty rivers and canals, and over 100 islands, St. Petersburg is neither European nor Russian, but the best of both. Combining the imperial palaces and dark rivers of Russia and the geometric layout and planned architecture of Europe, it's no wonder this great city is called the Venice of the North.

Setting the Scene

To get ready for your armchair stay in St. Petersburg, first think about the time of year you'd like to visit. In the winter, lots of blankets and candles set the scene. In the cold months, the Neva freezes hard enough that people walk across; sledding and ice skating are popular. Find an ice skating rink, go sledding or cross-country skiing to really become a part of your St. Petersburg experience.

If you decide to have a summer or spring weekend, do as they do in St. Petersburg, and hit the beach. If you would rather stay inside, celebrate the "Musical Spring in St. Petersburg" with musical selections from any number of Petersburg native musicians. Other musical festivities include "The White Nights Swing, Jazz Festival" and "Stars of the White Nights, Classical Music Festival"; both concerts are a part of the celebration of the long summer nights, when the sun hardly sets and it never really gets dark.

If you have children and would like to entertain them as they do in St. Petersburg, give a puppet show! There are three puppet theaters throughout the city, one of which does more *noire* puppet shows, meant for adults.

Inside your home, to capture the feel of this setting, get out your chess board, *Matryoshka* nesting dolls (usually painted red), and best china. Set out any wooden trinkets, bowls, or clocks, as well as any red blankets, pillows, or throws you may have. Artwork by Ilya Repin, a realist painter, Dmitriy Levitsy, Orest Kiprenskiy, and Kary Bryullov, or photos of St. Petersburg set out on tables or hung on walls or windows should help the mood.

Decorating eggs at Easter is an elaborate ritual originating in the Ukraine. Eggs make beautiful decorations for any season when placed in a bowl. For this you will need a pencil, beeswax, a tablespoon, candle, a stylus with a hollow point (found in art stores), raw white eggs, and different bowls of egg dye (yellow, orange, red, and black).

Holding the pencil steady in one hand and rotating the egg in the other, draw a light pencil line around the egg lengthwise. Starting again at the top of the egg, draw another line crossing the first at right angles, dividing the egg into quarters. Now, draw a third line around the middle of the egg. Load the stylus with the beeswax, and hold the point briefly over the lit candle. Test the flow of the wax on a piece of paper before drawing lines of wax over the pencil marks. Draw new lines with the stylus across the open areas, dividing each area into six triangles. Place the egg in the teaspoon, dipping it into the yellow dye, then gentle pat off the excess dye. Draw small circles in alternate triangles with the stylus, then dip the egg into the orange dye. Pat dry, and place a dot of wax in the center of each circle. Dip into the red dye, then pat dry. Finally, draw diagonal lines in each of the remaining triangles, then dip the egg into the black dye. You should have a beautifully decorated egg that will keep for a long time if kept out of sunlight.

Books

Fyodor Dostoevsky is best known for his novel, *Crime and Punishment.* Based in St. Petersburg, like many of his novels, it is the story of the murder of a moneylender. Dostoevsky also wrote *The Brothers Karamozov, The Idiot, Notes from the Underground, The Adolescent, The Possessed,* and *The Gambler. Memoirs of the Dead* is the faithful story of Dostoevsky's four years in a fortress-prison of Omsk. A warning though: Most of his novels are dark and filled with political and sociological messages. If you are looking for something shorter to read during the weekend, *Notes from the Underground, The Double,* and *The Eternal Husband* are short stories that make for faster reading.

St. Petersburg native Alexander Pushkin has long been considered the father of modern Russian literature. Pushkin is most noted for his poetry, including *The Clouds, The Dagger, Epistle to the Prince of Orange, I Have Lived to Bury My Desires,* and *The Bronze Horseman,* a tribute to St. Petersburg's Great Flood of 1824. Reading some aloud might set exactly the right tone.

In addition to Pushkin, St. Petersburg produced an amazing number of poets during the first decade of the twentieth century. They include Aleksandr Blok, Andrei Bely *(Petersburg),* and Anna Akhmatova *(Poems Without a Hero and Selected Poems* is one of the best collections available). Joseph Brodsky (1940–1996), who won the Nobel Prize for literature in 1987, was a protégé of poet Anna Akhmatova. Brodsky was forced to emigrate after years of the government's refusal to print any of his books of poetry, which include *Elegy for John Donne*

Russian Phrases to Use Liberally

Yes = *Da* (da)

No = *Net* (nyet)

Please, You are welcome = *Pozhaluysta* (pazhalsta)

Thank you = *Spasibo* (spaseeba)

Good day = *Dobryy den* (dobree dyen)

How are you? = *Kak dela?* (kak dyela)

How do you say in Russian . . . ? *Kak po-russki... ?* (kak pa-rooskee) and Other Poems, Selected Poems, To Urania, A Part of Speech, and *Less Than One.*

For light reading, try *Dead Meat* by Philip Kerr, a detective story set in St. Petersburg; the historical novel, *The Master of Petersburg* by J. M. Coetzee; or *Dispatch from a Cold Country* by Robert Cullen. Cullen writes of murder, greed, high-stakes crime, and corruption in today's Russia.

Videos

One of the best things to do on your armchair adventure is to have an evening of entertainment in the St. Petersburg fashion by going to the opera or the ballet. Dress in your best, and head to the "opera house"—a quiet room with a good VCR or DVD player and a copy of your favorite production. Libraries carry the PBS broadcasts of most operas, and many video stores carry operas in the Musical or Foreign sections. If you haven't seen an opera or ballet before, or aren't sure you'll like it, try a popular ballet like *The Nutcracker* or an opera like *Kismet.* If you are up for the adventure, try *Boris Gudenov.*

If it's art you crave, some of the best cultural entertainment available is the "Hermitage Masterpieces" video series, produced by Studio Quart. There are eighteen programs in the series, including nine videos of the most prestigious pieces of art ever collected together. The Hermitage Museum in St. Petersburg houses Europe's largest collection of Picasso's Cubist paintings and large galleries of Matisse and Gauguin, as well as Rembrandt, Raphael, da Vinci, Rubens, El Greco, and Renoir. In addition, displays of sculpture, decorative arts, and the architecture of the buildings themselves are on view in more than 400 rooms. The videos include commentary on the life of Peter the Great, the founder of St. Petersburg, and life in Russia during his time. You can find these in most public libraries or by calling (800) 847-7733.

Other great movies for this weekend adventure:

The Yellow Ticket (1918). Anna Mirrel, a young Jewish girl in Czarist Russia, is forced to degrade herself in order to visit her father, who is ill. She obtains a yellow passport, indicating that she is a prostitute, and travels to St. Petersburg, where she finds her father has been killed. In St. Petersburg she encounters a young journalist and tells him of the crimes the state perpetuates against it citizens. The pair are arrested after her remarks are published, and Anna must decide whether or not to submit to the desires of the sinister chief of police in order to obtain their freedom.

The Idiot (1958). Dostoevsky's novel is brought to life in this film about a young prince returning to St. Petersburg after a stay in an asylum in Switzerland. Prince Myshkin falls for Aglaya, the daughter of a wealthy man, but is in love with Nastasia. The choices he is forced to make are the focus of this tragedy.

Tschaikovsky (1971). In Russian, with English subtitles, directed by Talankin, *Tschaikovsky* is a film about the great composer's life and works.

Backstage at the Kirov (1984). A look at the famed St. Petersburg ballet (called *Kirov* during the Soviet era, now Mariinskiy Ballet), one of the best classical dance troupes in the world. One of this troupe's most astounding early choreographers, Marius Petipa, inspired such dancers as Matilda Kshesinskaya, Vaslav Nijinsky, and Anna Pavlova.

Anna Karenina (1997). Filmed in and around St. Petersburg, this love story is based on Tolstoy's novel of the same name. Stefan and Dolly Oblonsky have had a spat, and Stefan asks his sister, Anna Karenina, to help mend the rift. Anna's companion on the train is Countess Vronsky, whose dashing son Colonel Vronsky sweeps Anna off her feet. Their meetings must be discreet, as Anna as a husband and small son. With Sophie Marceau, James Fox, and Sean Bean.

If you want to see a Russian film, check out *Burnt by the Sun* (1994), directed by Nikita Mikhalkov, which won the Academy

Award for Best Foreign Language Film and the Grand Prize of the Jury Award at Cannes. Granted, it takes place outside Moscow, but it is a poignant depiction of the tragedy of Stalinism, with gorgeous cinematography. Also check out the work of Grigoriy Kozintsev. He was one of the leading Russian directors from Lenfilm Studios in St. Petersburg. Kozintsev directed, among other films, *Hamlet* (1964) and *King Lear* (1970), both of which marked his success in the West. These films also featured music composed by Shostakovitch.

*M*usic

Russia, and St. Petersburg in particular, has a history of producing classical musical geniuses and innovators, including Tchaikovsky, Prokofiev, and Shostakovitch. One good way to get a taste of the caliber of these artists is to check out a compilation entitled *Anthologie de la melodie russa et sovietique,* produced by the French Harmonia Mundi. Or you can listen to the many fine recordings of their symphonies.

Music from the Court of St. Petersburg (Volume II) includes works from Teplov, Kozlovsky, Kurakina and Siniavina, Rimsky-Korsakov, Borodin, Mussorgsky, and Tchaikovsky. It is one of the best collections available of music that surely would have graced the court of Catherine the Great.

Aleksandr Borodin was not only a great Russian composer but also a physician and professor of chemistry. Borodin composed the operas *Prince Igor* and *Kismet,* as well as *Symphony #1 in E-flat minor* and *Symphony #2 in B minor.* Modest Mussorgsky is best known for his operas *Boris Gudenov, Pictures at an Exhibition,* and *Khovanshchina.* You might enjoy any of these works based on Russian folk music, or perhaps Nikolai Rimsky-Korsakov's opera *Scheherazade.* And don't neglect Igor Stravinsky, who is best known for *The Firebird Suite (L'oiseau de feu),* and *The Rite of Spring (Le sacre du printemps),* which caused riots in its first public performance in Paris.

Food

The St. Petersburg diet is hefty, due to the long, cold winters. The day begins with tea, and a sweet roll or bread and butter. There's a simple lunch at noon, usually fish or meat and a vegetable with a small dessert, followed by dinner, the main meal of the day. Dinner always begins with a small assortment of hors d'oeuvres, accompanied by vodka and caviar, followed by soup. A fish course comes next, followed by a meat course, both accompanied by vegetables, and finally dessert. An evening tea ends the day, with cold cuts, cheeses, and fruit offered.

The best book available on various menus and serving suggestions is *The Art of Russian Cuisine* by Anne Volokh. Volokh provides menus, recipes, the history of food in Russia, and suggestions for holiday meals. Russians are very hospitable, making sure that guests are never wanting for food and drink; every meal consists of enough food to satisfy the hungriest guest!

Here I give menus for a main meal. For the appetizer course, serve smoked salmon, caviar, pickled vegetables, and/or *pirozhki*. A wonderful recipe for pirozhki is in *The Art of Russian Cuisine,* which includes diagrams and very clear instructions on how to make this slightly complicated but delectable concoction.

Kholodnyi Borsht

COLD BEET SOUP

If you want hot soup, heat up before adding the sour cream and eliminate the cucumbers.

2 tablespoons butter	pepper to taste
½ cup chopped onions	8 cups beef or vegetable stock

Caviar Chat

There are a number of caviars available, from the expensive Sevruga Caviar to the cheaper, but still good, American Salmon Caviar. The best caviars are made from sturgeon, have a dark gray to black color, and are made with very little salt. Salmon caviar, which is sharper in taste and less expensive that sturgeon caviar, is the reddish-gold colored caviar that is seen in delicatessen areas of the grocery store. But read the labels carefully to know what kind of caviar you are buying—some manufacturers have been known to dye salmon caviar black!

Serve caviar in a glass or on ice on a metal platter, making sure that the caviar is close to room temperature before serving (a little cooler than warmer is best). Serve with small triangles of lightly toasted, thinly sliced bread. Some connoisseurs prefer the bread very lightly buttered. For those who do not insist on the singular flavor of caviar, make sure that there is lemon juice and/or chopped chives in small dishes on the side.

1½ lbs. cooked beets, drained
   (may be canned)
¼ cup red wine vinegar
1 teaspoon sugar
2 peeled, chopped tomatoes
4 medium potatoes, peeled and halved
2 teaspoons salt

4 sprigs parsley
½ cup chopped fresh dill
3 bay leaves
6 teaspoons sour cream
2 cups peeled and sliced cucumbers
6 tablespoons chopped scallions
3 hard-boiled eggs, peeled and sliced

Melt the butter over medium heat in a large soup pot. Add the onions and cook until tender, about 5 minutes. Stir in the next seven ingredients. Pour in ½ cup of stock, put the lid on, and simmer for 50 minutes. Pour the remaining stock into the pot as well as the parsley, dill, and bay leaves. Simmer for ½ hour.

Remove from heat and refrigerate for at least an hour. Just before serving, strain 1 cup of the soup and mix it with the sour cream in a small bowl. Pour the sour cream mixture back into the tureen and mix well. Stir in the cucumbers and scallions. Serve in chilled bowls topped with the eggs. Serves 6.

Kuritsa Otvarnaia

POACHED CHICKEN

This very simple preparation goes well with a variety of other courses.

1 3½ lb. whole roasting chicken, washed
water to cover
1 bunch fresh dill, cleaned
1 teaspoon salt

1 onion, cut in half
2 carrots, cut into chunks
2 potatoes, cut into chunks

Place the chicken in a large, heavy-bottomed pot breast side down, and cover with cold water. Bring to a boil, add the remaining ingredients, cover, and return to a boil. When it begins to boil, reduce heat and simmer for 30–35 minutes, or until the chicken is cooked. Remove the chicken from the pan and carve into serving pieces. Serve with the vegetables. Serves 4.

Blinchikis Povidlom

DESSERT PANCAKES

Chocolate lovers, consider using chocolate milk instead of regular milk.

1½ cups flour

2 cups milk

2 eggs, separated

1 tablespoon sugar

½ teaspoon salt

3 tablespoons vegetable oil

4–6 tablespoons unsalted butter, melted

Jam of your choosing

½ cup sugar mixed with 1 tablespoon cinnamon

Put the flour in a large mixing bowl and slowly mix in the milk. Beat in the egg yolks, sugar, salt, and oil with an electric mixer. After mixing thoroughly, set the batter aside on the counter for at least 3 hours.

When you are ready to make the pancakes, beat the egg whites in a large bowl with a whisk until soft peaks form, then fold the mixture into the batter.

Preheat the oven to 250°F. With a pastry brush, lightly coat a 5- to 6-inch crepe pan or skillet with 1 teaspoon of butter. Pour in ½ cup of the batter, tilting the pan to spread it evenly. Cook until the pancake is golden on the bottom. Turn it over with a spatula, and cook for about ½ the time you did the first side. Place on a plate and keep warm in the oven. Repeat until batter is used up.

When pancakes are finished, spread the jam on one side of each pancake. Fold into half and then half again, and brown in remaining butter in the pan. Sprinkle with the sugar-cinnamon mixture and serve warm. Serves 4.

— *Teresa Coronado*

Bottoms Up

No Russian meal would be complete without the requisite vodka. There are many kinds and flavors of Russian vodka; try a variety by buying tiny bottles of the vodkas that look the most appealing to you. Vodka is usually taken during the beginning of the meal. Vodka, which has been known in Russia for at least 1,000 years, comes in many varieties and flavors, as well as a variety of strengths; Smirnoff, Stolichnaya, Starka, Petrovskaia, and Okhatnichia are a few of the named Russian vodkas on the market. Flavored (or infused) vodkas are also available in liquor stores; they range from honey, apple, and pear to mint, vanilla, and clove. Flavors are combined, some-times as many as forty flavors at once!

To make your own flavored vodka, select a straight vodka and add your favorite flavor. For instance, to make a lemon vodka, add the rind of a lemon to 1 quart of vodka, reseal, and leave at room temperature for about a week. Be sure to strain well and chill before serving. Combinations of herbs and spices are said to be medic-inal; using aromatherapy (my favorite book on aromatherapy is *Aromatherapy Through the Seasons* by Paula Bousquet and Judith Fitzsimmons) with your before- or after-dinner drink can actually be healthful!

A Passage to India

Setting the Scene

AHHH, INDIA . . . redolent of spices, retina-searing saris, and the interwoven tangle of myth and religion. I, for one, believe this to be the perfect recipe for a great escape. The subcontinent is a place of mystery and vast differences. Many languages, religions, and peoples make up this land. A weekend in India provides the perfect opportunity not only to embrace these differences but to celebrate and even savor them.

I am a confessed Indiaphile—I love the literature, the music, the food, and the people of this magical place, and I have spent the last few years exploring these aspects. I had the help of a boy from Bombay; here we'll share our trade secrets with you.

A trip to India needn't break the budget, but I recommend starting with a trip to a bargain import gourmet store like Cost Plus. For $20, you can buy Nag Champa incense, scented with the very breath of the gods, a package of chai tea, spices, lentils, scarves, candles, and even decorative accents such as brass bells or mirrors. When you buy spices, make sure you get some saffron. Many big cities throughout the United States boast sari shops and Indian food markets. You can find not only items to create atmosphere, and Indian spices, but also very inexpensive Indian video and audiotapes to enhance the ambiance.

The regions of pre-Partition, Colonial India included "Mother India herself," Nepal, Pakistan, Bangladesh, and Sri Lanka. India contains every possible climate, from the driest desert to the lushest jungle to the highest mountains in the world. This is most definitely a land of extremes; it has a plethora of cultures, customs, and cuisines to match this diversity. One great theme for an Indian weekend is a survey of the vast array of Indian music. Another is cuisines of its various regions. There is a Sanskrit saying that "the guest is truly your god," which reflects the importance Indians place on hospitality. Whatever you decide to do, be sure it includes a meal to which you invite others.

Books

I am a huge fan of contemporary Indian fiction, so my books suggestions all fall into that category. One great lazy way to "visit" India for a weekend would be to order Indian food to go and curl up with any of these:

A Suitable Boy by Vikram Seth, a tome that is often compared to Proust's *Remembrance of Things Past,* was the book that started my obsession with Indian writers. Indeed, the scents, sounds, and riot of color that is India are gathered here in 900 pages to be savored. I truly felt I had lived in India for a fortnight after finishing this masterpiece. It may take you longer than the weekend to read, but it is worth it.

Bharati Muhkerjee has been the harbinger of an impressive wave of post-Colonial writers from the subcontinent. My favorite of her books is *Jasmine,* an evocative tale of a sensual young woman's coming of age.

Chitra Divakaruni is nothing less than a marvel. She seemingly burst onto the scene with her poetry in the early 1990s while running a nonprofit organization to help battered Asian women and broken families. Brilliant and benevolent, her novels are essential reading for any vicarious passage to India: *The Arranged Marriage, Sister of My Heart,* and my favorite, *The Mistress of Spices.*

Salman Rushdie certainly drew the eyes of the world to Indian literature when he became the object of a *jihad,* a Muslim death sentence, when he published *The Satanic Verses.* He has written extensively, and now that he can move about without fear for his life, is part of the international glitterati. I love his *Moor's Last Sigh,* which takes place largely in Kerala, the humid, southern spice center of India.

Jhumpa Lahiri took home a Pulitzer for her first effort, *Interpreter of Maladies,* a collection of heartbreakingly beautiful short stories. She counts among her biggest fans no less than Amy Tan, who says it best: "Jhumpa Lahiri is the kind of writer who makes you want to grab the next person you see and say, 'Read this!'" Try a story or two before dinner.

Post-Colonial Indian writers fully arrived with the stunning debut of Arundhati Roy's *The God of Small Things.* This novel about the tragic lives of a pair of twins living in Karala, India captured the imagination of readers. Very nearly stream-of-consciousness, this unusual story has a Faulknerian scope and is equally mythological and magical. Roy is herself fascinating, an architect and BBC journalist who risked firing and controversy to fight the building of dams that devastate entire villages and regions of India.

The books mentioned here are widely available in bookstores. Two good online book sources for more indigenous fare include: Bagchee Associates (bagchee.com), which has a database of 1 million Indian book titles, and India Internet Book Fair (oscarindia.com).

Videos

Movies are essential to your immersion in all things Indian. India's movie industry based in Bombay (now known as Mombai) and known as Bollywood, has the biggest movie production business outside of Los Angeles. Indians love big, splashy films with love songs; dance sequences, and bindi'd love goddesses. I advise renting any of these videos to capture the heart and soul of India. Pop them in the VCR and curl up with a cool *lassi!* If you need some education on Bollywood fare, try logging on to Planet Bollywood.com.

If you want more serious fare, you must begin with *Gandhi* (1982), Ben Kingsley's tour de force performance of the true life of the man many regard as India's savior. *A Passage to India* (1984), the E. M. Forster novel brought to the screen by the producing team of Merchant-Ivory, would also be a great selection.

If you are looking for some spice in your weekend, consider the sexy glamfest *Kama Sutra*. In this 1996 movie directed by Mira Nair, a lowly sixteenth-century servant seduces the husband of her childhood friend using the ancient art of seduction described in the Indian book of love, the *Kama Sutra*. Definitely not for children. Subtitled.

The "father of Indian cinema" is Satyajit Ray, whose films for decades were very cultured and extremely experimental compared with Bollywood's soap-operatic fare. His masterful trilogy of a Bengali boy's life from birth through manhood appears in the award-winning films *Pather Panchali* (1955), *Aparajito* (1956), and *The World of Apu* (1959). All have subtitles.

Also worth renting, if only for historical reasons, is 1994's *Bandit Queen,* directed by Sheekhar Kapur. This film is based on the real-life story of Devi Phoolan, who was sold into marriage at age eleven. Defying convention, she ran away from her much older husband to join a gang of bandits and eventually brought the Indian government to its knees.

Music

The different music styles of India can at first be overwhelming to a Westerner. Start with the classical and move on from there. I began with tabla, ragas, flutes, and sitars. Once I got going with a few listenings, I noticed that Western music lost some of its luster for me. While that has passed, the exotic music did somehow fill me with the sense of India and made me curious about the people, history, and tradition that made these strange and wonderful sounds.

Indian music goes back almost 2,000 years and is a blend of races and cultures, both indigenous and foreign, Persian in particular. Indian music is unlike any other musical form. It rests on two musical bases—*raga* (the basis of Indian melody) and *tala* (the basis of Indian rhythm). Ideally, the Western listener is requested to forget counterpoint and harmony in favor of an appreciation of rhythmic and melodic patterns.

North Indian music is popularly known as Hindustani music and South Indian as Karnatic; their origin is the same, but the approach and style are quite different. To get a good sense, consider a compilation like *Flute and Sitar Music of India: Meditational Ragas.* If you are looking for some exposure to Indian folk

Indian Instruments

Indian music features a number of instruments that are seen nowhere else in the world, including the *sitar,* a guitar-like stringed instrument that has been in use for about 700 years, and the *sarangi,* which is played with a bow and has four main strings and as many as forty resonant strings, and which is most often used to accompany singers. And anyone who has ever heard Indian music has heard *tabla,* the two hand drums that are played as accompaniment to North Indian music and dance. The *jal tarang* is a xylophone-type instrument made of different sized china bowls filled with varying levels of water and played with two sticks.

music, consider *All the Best from India.* Or try something from
Ravi Shankar, the most renowned sitar player of all time, who
was made popular in the West by the Beatles. Both his *India's
Master Musician* and *The Sounds of India* are worth listening to.

Recently I have fallen in love with Indian techno music,
particularly my nearly worn-out CD of Talvin Singh's *Anoka:
Soundz from the Asian Underground.* And I can't get through a
week without listening to my collection of wacky
compilations of Bollywood movie scores, such as my
personal favorite, *Bombay the Hard Way,* with the
searingly sexy track "Fear of a Brown Planet."

Food

Indian cuisine is extremely varied, and, like that of
China, is very regionally based. Kashmiri cuisine,
originating in the extreme north of India near the Hi-
malayas, features much more meat than most of the
rest of India. Lamb, goat, chicken, and freshwater fish
are favored, while saffron and chilies grown in the region are often used to spice food. A meal is followed
by a large serving of fresh fruit such as strawberries,
cherries, or apples, which are raised in the plentiful orchards
of the region, which grow here due to the cooler climes.

The Punjab is northernmost India, joining Pakistan, Tibet, and Kashmir to the south. This is a beautiful area featuring old Moghul palaces that are the favorite settings for Bollywood films. Peopled by Hindus, Sikhs, Muslims, Buddhists, and Jains, Punjab offers clothing, food, and décor that are colorful and romantic. It is said that the Punjabi people are robust people with robust appetites and that their food reflects this in quantity and style. This is the home of the renowned tandoori cooking,

which had become one of the most popular cuisines in the world. Tandoori are huge earthen ovens in the ground that are heated from below with coal fires. Marinated meats, fish, chicken, lamb, and anything else take on an incomparable, rich flavor. This area also has wildly popular breads, now available in prepackaged varieties in many grocery stores—including parathas, rotis, and naan. Any proper Punjabi meal should also be accompanied by lassi, a sweet or salted dairy-based drink.

The Moghuls ruled India for centuries and left behind a rich legacy, especially in the cuisine of the capital city, New Delhi. The word *Moghul* translates to "fit for royalty," and the food reflects this heritage; it is comprised of rich sauces, gravies, but-ter-infused curries, and other elements replete with romanti-cism. This is the "fancy food" of India and remains popular hundreds of years after the fall of their empire. A rose petal *kulfi* or tart fruits *shorba* is the Moghul flavor ideal.

The Bengalis' greatest gift to India's food heritage is a huge array of sweets and snacks including *gulab jamuns,* to name one of the tantalizing treats available in this highly creative and sweet-toothed region. You will find a repast of desserts made from scorched and boiled milk in every Bengali home.

Bengalis don't eat meat, as they are largely Hindu and therefore vegetarian, but they do consume a great deal of fish, which they cook in every possible way. The spices here are also very different and their "trade secret" is the use of *panch-phoron,* a five-spice mixture that includes *zeera, kalaunji, saun,* and mustard seeds. Perhaps the best way to explain the Bengali way is that the flavors are a mixture of sweet and spicy—not to be missed!

The Maharashtra region includes Bombay and all the low-lying and coastal areas of southwest and central India. This cui-sine combines flavor-infused vegetables, utilizing the enormous variety of produce grown in the region, with meat; specialties in-clude fiery fish curries and succulent meat dishes. Two "mi-crocuisines" found here are the very exotic Konkani and Malwani, representing the tastes of the coasts, with their abundant variety of seafood. Rice is most definitely the staple food of this cuisine. All meals are served with boiled rice or *bhakris,* a soft flour cake. Grated coconut adorns many dishes, and other oils are eschewed in favor of peanut oil. *Shreekhand* is a thick, sweetened yogurt of this region. Spiced with cardamom and saffron, it is a staple at Indian weddings.

Most Indians eat with their hands. However, the more Westernized people now resort to knives, forks, and spoons. Generally speaking, most Indian meals are communal, and all of the food is placed in the center of the table at the same time; there is no concept of courses. That way, people help themselves to whatever they want, whenever they want. In much of South India, the food comes arranged on metal platters called *thalis,* with liquid dishes placed in small bowls *(katoris)*. These platters have everything from *samosas* to sweets served all at once.

The meal presented here includes several favorites from around India: one appetizer, a soup, one main course, a side dish or vegetarian entree, a *raita* (yogurt-based salad), a dessert and a recipe for lassi, the wonderful Indian beverage. Fill in with storebought chutneys, and don't forget the rice—preferably Basmati.

If you are looking for cookbooks to augment the meal here, consider anything by Madhur Jaffrey, especially *An Invitation to Indian Cooking.* Jaffrey is the main popularizer of Indian food in the United States, and she knows how to adjust for American tastes and ingredients. Also consider *The Foods of India* by Karen Anand, Jennifer Brennan, and Wendy Hutton. It is a wonderful overview.

Samosas

These are great as appetizers or snacks. This is adapted from an Indian recipe—the egg roll wrappers make a great covering and the store-bought curry powder cuts down on time and ingredients.

Filling

1 tablespoon butter or *ghee*

1 onion, finely diced

2 cloves garlic, crushed

$\frac{1}{2}$ lb. lean ground beef

1 medium potato, peeled, cooked, and diced

$\frac{1}{4}$ cup frozen peas

$\frac{1}{2}$ inch piece ginger, grated

2 teaspoons curry powder

$\frac{1}{2}$ teaspoon chili powder

$\frac{1}{2}$ teaspoon turmeric

salt and pepper to taste

1 tablespoon fresh mint, chopped

3 tablespoons water

1 tablespoon lemon juice

1 pkg. egg roll wrappers

peanut oil for deep frying

chutney of your choice

Melt the butter in a large frying pan, add the onion and garlic, and sauté over medium heat until onion is limp, about 5 minutes. Add all the rest of the filling ingredients except water and lemon juice, and sauté until just cooked through, about 5 minutes.

Add water and cook until water has evaporated. Remove from the heat and add the lemon juice. Stir well and let cool.

Cut the egg roll wrappers into 1³/₄-inch strips. To prepare the samosas, turn one end of the strips over to make a triangular-shaped pocket, then turn again in the opposite direction. Fill the opening with a spoonful of the ground beef mixture, and continue folding until the whole strip has been used and a triangular-shaped pastry results. Seal the end with water or a paste made from flour and water.

Heat oil for deep frying to fairly hot and fry the samosas, several at a time, until golden and crisp. Serve piping hot with chutney. Makes 3 dozen.

Dahl

Dahl is a legume soup that is eaten by itself or mixed with rice. *Garam masala* is a spice mixture that can be bought at an Indian store or made at home using an Indian cookbook.

3 tablespoons dried mung beans

3 tablespoons dried pigeon peas

3 tablespoons yellow split peas

3 tablespoons green split peas

3 tablespoons dried chick peas

7 cups chicken or vegetable stock

1 teaspoon turmeric

1 tablespoon dried coriander

1 tablespoon grated ginger root

1 teaspoon salt

4 oz. fresh spinach, washed and coarsely chopped

2 tablespoons butter or ghee

2 teaspoons cumin seeds

1 tablespoon minced fresh green chilies

¹/₄ teaspoon cayenne

¹/₂ teaspoon garam masala

water

Wash the beans and peas and place in a bowl. Pour hot water to cover and allow to sit for 1 hour. Drain.

In a large soup pot, combine the legumes with the next five ingredients. Bring to a boil, then reduce heat and simmer, covered, for 1½ hours, stirring occasionally.

Remove the pot from the heat and beat mixture with a beater till the soup is smooth. Return to heat, add the spinach, and cook until wilted, about 5 minutes.

In a small frying pan, melt the butter or ghee. Add the cumin seeds, chilies, cayenne, and garam masala, and allow to become fragrant and hot, stirring constantly, about 2 minutes. Add a bit of water to make a thin paste, stirring constantly. Pour into the soup. Serves 6.

Aloo Baigan Sabji

CURRIED EGGPLANT AND POTATOES

2 small green chilies

¼ cup shredded unsweetened coconut

½-inch piece ginger

½ teaspoon garam masala

⅓ cup water, approximately

3 tablespoons peanut oil, approximately

1 teaspoon mustard powder

½ tablespoon cumin

⅛ teaspoon curry powder

4 large potatoes, peeled, boiled, and diced

1 teaspoon turmeric

1 tablespoon coriander powder

1 small eggplant, peeled and diced

1 teaspoon salt

1 teaspoon black pepper

1 tablespoon lemon juice

Place green chilies, coconut, ginger, garam masala, and water in food processor or blender and process till smooth. Put aside.

Heat 2 tablespoons oil in a large frying pan. Add mustard, cumin, and curry, and sauté, stirring constantly, until fragrant, about 1 minute. Add potatoes and sauté, stirring often, for 5 minutes, adding more oil if needed to keep from sticking. Add reserved chilies mixture, turmeric, coriander, and eggplant. Simmer until the liquid has evaporated and eggplant is tender, adding more water if needed, about 15 minutes. Stir in lemon juice. Serves 4.

Bombay Beef with Curry Butter

This calls for steaming the beef, which is not a traditional preparation in the United States. But it is delicious. It requires a large steamer that will hold the steaks.

Curry Butter

¼ lb. butter	1 small green chili, seeded
2 thin slices ginger	2 tablespoon curry powder
1 shallot	½ teaspoon turmeric
2 garlic cloves	1 tablespoon lemon juice

Steaks

1 stalk lemongrass, chopped	water for steaming
1 inch piece fresh ginger, thinly sliced	4 steaks, 1-inch thick
15 whole black peppercorns	salt and freshly ground pepper to taste

To make the Curry Butter, put all the ingredients in a blender or food processor and blend until smooth. Set aside.

Place the lemongrass, ginger, and peppercorns in the bottom of a large steamer. Add water up to the bottom of the steamer. Boil on high 2 minutes. While water is boiling, salt and pepper the steaks. Add the steaks to the steamer, and steam them for 3 minutes or until done to your taste. Serve with Curry Butter on the side. Serves 4.

Tamatar Raita

TOMATO AND YOGURT SALAD

2 ripe tomatoes, minced

½ medium onion, minced

1 small green chili, minced

1 cup plain yogurt (can be nonfat)

Stir all ingredients in a medium bowl and refrigerate for ½ hour to allow flavors to blend. Stir again before serving. Serves 4.

Kheer

This is a luscious dessert.

½ cup uncooked white rice

½ cup water

4 cups milk (can be low-fat)

¼ cup currants

1 cup brown sugar

1 teaspoon cardamom seeds, crushed
   and outer husk discarded

⅛ teaspoon ginger powder

¼ cup shredded blanched almonds

Wash and drain the rice. Place in a medium saucepan and add the water. Soak for ½ hour.

Place pan over medium heat and boil the rice until the water evaporates, about 10 minutes. Add the milk and simmer on low for 1½ hour, stirring frequently to prevent sticking. When rice mixture is creamy add currants, sugar, cardamom seeds, and almonds. Mix well and serve warm. Serves 4.

Lassi

Rosewater is available at Indian markets and at specialty food stores.

1 vanilla pod, seeds removed

4 cardamom pods, seeds removed and husks discarded

4 cups nonfat plain yogurt

5 tablespoons brown sugar

1 tablespoon rosewater

nutmeg to taste

Crush the vanilla and cardamom seeds. Blend 2 cups yogurt, vanilla, cardamom, and brown sugar in a food processor or blender until smooth. Pour into bowl and add remaining yogurt and rosewater. Stir well. Serve in individual glasses and sprinkle with nutmeg. Serves 4.

—Brenda Knight

Fun and Feasting in China

Setting the Scene

CHINA is an immense country, with many different languages, cultures, traditions, and types of food. One way to begin to narrow down the prospects for creating an armchair weekend is to plan your weekend around one of the traditional Chinese holidays. You might want to incorporate some of the traditions and decorations mentioned here into your armchair weekend.

CHINESE NEW YEAR

The big daddy of them all is Chinese New Year, which begins on the second new moon after the shortest day of the year, December 21, and lasts about two weeks. In Western calendars, this means the holiday begins sometime in late January or early February. Prior to the big event, the house is cleaned from stem to stern. On New Year's Eve, families get together for a banquet. What is served varies from region to region, but throughout the country, the last course that is eaten is fish, because fish in Chinese *(yu)* sounds like "great plenty." Because red signifies good luck, all the children in the family receive red envelopes filled with money, and the parents write short poems called "spring couplets" on red paper that are then placed in the doorway of the house to greet the New Year. Plates of oranges are placed around the house for good luck, and blooming plants are placed inside and out. The whole family stays up late, playing games, telling stories, and making wishes.

On the first day, strings of firecrackers are ignited to welcome in the New Year and chase any evil spirits away. The family dresses in new clothes and visits relatives bearing gifts of tangerines and oranges for good luck. Everyone eats long noodles, which signify longevity; sugared melon, which stands for good health; and lotus seeds, because lotus *(lian zi)* sounds like the expression "lots of children." In the North, folks eat *jiao zi,* steamed dumplings filled with meat or vegetables, while in the South, they prefer them filled with coconut and peanuts.

On the fifteenth day of the New Year comes the Lantern Festival, in which people parade through the streets carrying lanterns of all types and sizes—paper, silk, bamboo, from tiny lights to lanterns as big as a building (in the North where it is very cold, some are even carved of ice!). This is where the tradition of the Chinese New Year's parade comes from. It was believed that the lights from the lanterns helped the wandering ghosts of the ancestors find their way home. This is when the 100-foot dragon wakes from hibernation and dances through the streets, symbolizing power and goodness as it chases after the sun, the source of its strength. Generally speaking, all business comes to a standstill during these two weeks, which are spent visiting friends and relatives.

CLEAR BRIGHTNESS FESTIVAL

This takes place on April 4, 5, or 6, and is held in honor of a family's ancestors. The family gathers together and then goes to the graveside of their ancestors, where they tidy the graves and paste little bits of red paper on top of the tombstones to give the ancestors a roof over their heads. The living relatives then set out all kinds of tasty food for the ancestors (it is believed that the afterlife is like the world of the living and food is required) and proceed to have a picnic themselves at the graveside. After eating, everyone sits silently with their eyes closed, remembering good times with their relatives who have passed on. Then everyone, especially children, gets up to fly kites. Kites were originally used in China thousands of years ago to send messages between armies. Later they were incorporated into festivals, particularly springtime ones. They come in all shapes, sizes, and colors.

DRAGON BOAT FESTIVAL

This race using dragon boats takes place on the fifth day of the fifth lunar month (usually held in early summer in the United States). It commemorates the search for Qu Yuan, China's earliest known poet, who disappeared by the banks of the river more than 2,000 years ago after his advice on how to keep peace was ignored. The townspeople got into their boats to try and find him but never did, so they threw rice into the water to feed his ghost. But, says the legend, Qu Yuan never got to eat the food because a dragon with the horns of a deer, the eyes of a rabbit, the scales of a fish, and the claws of a hawk kept getting there first. Finally a fisherman who was having no luck heard Qu Yuan's hungry cries, and asked Qu Yuan what he should do. "Seal the rice with bamboo leaves and tie the bundle with green, red, white, yellow, and black thread. That will scare the dragon off." From then on, the fisherman never heard from Qu Yuan again, but his nets were always full.

That's why today, sticky rice dumplings wrapped in bamboo leaves and tied with colored threads are eaten at the Dragon Boat Festival, and why children wear red, white, yellow, and black bracelets to ward off evil.

Traditionally the racers were all men, who rowed huge brightly colored dragon boats, up to 100 feet long, that have an open mouth at the bow and a tail at the stern. Today, women field their own teams too. Each team has a drummer who sets the pace for the paddlers. After the race, folks mill around, eating sticky rice bundles and roasted pine nuts, and watching martial arts demonstrations.

MOON FESTIVAL

This holiday is held on the fifteenth day of the eighth lunar month (usually mid-September according to the Western calendar) to celebrate the harvest and honor the moon. According to lore, centuries ago a Chinese woman, Chang E, flew to the moon and became the Goddess of the Palace of Great Cold. During the Moon Festival, Chang E will grant your wish, as long as it is something you have never told anyone else. The women in the family purchase round fruits like grapes, pomegranates, apples, and oranges, lay them on plates, and place them outside in their courtyards. Then families gather together outside to eat mooncakes, tell stories, gaze at the moon, and make secret wishes. Mooncakes are round like the moon and stand for togetherness and harmony. They are usually filled with sweet bean paste but some have coconut or lotus seed paste. They can be made, but are somewhat complicated; even people in China prefer to purchase them instead. You can find them at any Chinese food market in September.

Whether you plan your weekend around a festival or not, setting the scene can be easy. Think red and gold and take a trip to your local Chinatown to stock up on inexpensive paper lanterns, fans, kites, dragons, and other cut-outs that can be tacked to the walls. If you don't live near a Chinese community, you can order such items from *www.celebratechild.com.*

These days, folks in China wear Western clothes, but if you want to, you can buy traditional Chinese silk or shantung pajamas. They are very beautiful and can be worn over and over.

Don't Forget Chopsticks!

You can't create a Chinese weekend without chopsticks (called *kuai-zi,* "little fellows" in Chinese). No one knows exactly when the use of chopsticks originated, but it was in China thousands of years ago. During the twelfth century, they really caught on, due, it is said, to Confucius, who wrote that "an honorable man allows no knives at his table." Too dangerous—you could get angry and hurt someone. But be sure to use the Chinese ones—which are longer and straighter than Japanese. The only other allowed utensils are spoons; no knives or forks are ever used at the Chinese table. The no knife rule explains why all of Chinese cuisine is served bite-sized; it must be cut up before it reaches the table.

There are many superstitions that have grown up around chopsticks, including:

• Never point chopsticks at anyone or point them straight up vertically—it's very bad luck;

• If you get an uneven pair of chopsticks, you are going to miss a boat, train, or plane.

Chopsticks

My top choice for reading material for your adventure would be *Chinese Fairy Tales and Fantasies.* Edited by Moss Roberts, this is a wonderful translation of 100 brief fables from across twenty-five centuries, perfect for reading aloud.

If you like travel diaries, you might enjoy *Alone on the Great Wall* by William Lindesay, a touching story of an English runner who set out to run the 1,500 miles of the Great Wall and the adventures he had along the way. Or try *The River at the Center of the World,* the lyrical story of a journey up the Yangtzee by Simon Winchester.

*B*ooks

If you want a sense of what growing up in Shanghai was like in the late '50s and early '60s, read *Red Azalea* by Anchee Min, a compelling memoir of life during the Cultural Revolution. Min's early life was very trying, but she tells her story without anger or bitterness. Be warned, however: This is not "fun."

To get a sense of the hip style of modern China, you must get the lavishly illustrated *China Chic* by hotter-than-hot fashion designer Vivienne Tam. In it, she takes you on a visual tour of what has inspired her in China and Hong Kong, revealing both herself and the essence of modern Chinese design.

For a glimpse into the changing face of China, pick up *China: The Photographs of Lois Conner.* Conner is considered one of the greatest photographers shooting today. For the past fifteen years, she traveled alone throughout the vast country with a panoramic camera. This book is the testament to what she saw.

If you would like to get some sense of the poetry of China, try *The Clouds Should Know Me by Now: Buddhist Poet Monks of China,* edited by Red Pine. *Clouds* is a collection of Chinese Zen poetry, which is similar to the Japanese haiku in its spare style. This literary tradition has been practiced in China for centuries, but has only recently come to attention in the West.

Have a hankering for a novel? Don't miss *Waiting* by Ha Jin, which won a Pulitzer Prize in 2000. Deceptively simple, it is a deadly accurate peek into the lives of modern Chinese workers that reveals a tremendous amount about love, politics, and the Chinese psyche. For something a bit lighter, try Bette Boa Lord's *Spring Moon.* This is one of those thick, engrossing, page-turning paperbacks that spans the centuries (in this case the nineteenth and twentieth) and is full of colorful characters, political intrigue, and a compelling love story. Perfect for a weekend's entertainment.

To really get a sense of the country, consider a wonderful travelogue with the silly name of *Video Visits China*. It takes you across 2,000 miles of Chinese landscape from the Gobi Desert to the China Sea, and 4,000 years of history from the Great Wall to modern Beijing. It's available at *www.celebratechild.com*.

*V*ideos

To see incredible scenery and get a sense of history along with a passionate love story, check out the Chinese epic, *The Emperor and the Assassin* (1999), directed by Chen Kaige. It is the story of the man who united China in the third century and the woman who loved him (and his archrival). Chen Kaige also made another film considered to be one of the greatest epics of all times—the award-winning *Farewell My Concubine* (1993), which spans fifty years in the life of China by following two boys entering the Bejing Opera School. And for Chinese history on a grand visual scale, nothing beats Bernardo Bertolucci's *The Last Emperor* (1987), the story of Pu Yi, who was seven years old when the Communists dethroned him and took over China. Filmed inside the awesome Forbidden City itself, it offers a visually stunning look at this complex of 9,999 rooms where for centuries the royalty of China led their lives.

Another great film, not only for its historical depiction of the clash of the Communists with the Northern Chinese, but for its stunningly accurate look at the lives of women in China, is *Yellow Earth (Huang Tu Di,* 1984). Beautifully photographed, it offers a unique chance to hear the ethnic folk songs of the North, for the main character is a soldier sent to document these songs.

Two other great films for learning about Chinese life are *Xiu Xiu: The Sent Down Girl* (2000), directed by Joan Chen, which gives a very accurate if sad depiction of modern life, and *Raise the Red Lantern* (1991), which tells the tragic story of a concubine in Imperial times.

If you want something more lighthearted, consider two of world-famous Tawainese director Ang Lee's offerings: *The Wedding Banquet* (1993), the hilarious story of a gay Chinese man trying to deal with his parents' marriage expectations, and *Eat, Drink, Man, Woman* (1994), a heartfelt yet funny film that uses food as the metaphor for love in a Chinese family.

On the action side are the incredibly popular Hong Kong films. They are each full of violence—some subdued, others comic book-like, and still others extremely bloody. The best actor to watch in this genre, for fun and amazement, is Jackie

Chan. He does all his own stunts, and his films are the least violent of the type. Some of the best, which have all been dubbed, are *Rumble in the Bronx* (1996), *Legend of Drunken Master* (1994), *Crime Story* (1993), *Supercop* (1992), and *Operation Condor* (1991). Don't miss the closing credits where you get to watch the stunt outtakes.

The best director for these types of action films is John Woo. He revels in guns and violence and the idea that there are truly few differences between police and criminals. In the '90s he made quite a few films in the United States, but his best work comes out of Hong Kong. The action has to be seen to be believed, and the guns never seem to run out of bullets. His best are the lighter *Once a Thief* (1997), *Hard-Boiled* (1992), *Bullet in the Head* (1990), *The Killer* (1989), and *Heroes Shed No Tears* (1985).

For the ultimate martial arts epic, run out and rent *Crouching Tiger, Hidden Dragon* (2000). Incredibly choreographed, with breathtaking cinematography and music, this is Ang Lee's take on Hong Kong martial arts films. The thinking person's action movie.

Music

Chinese music is generally an acquired taste for the Western ear. If you are new to it, you might want to consider the anthologies *Once Upon a Time in China: The Best of Chinese Film Music* or *China Meditation.* Both are quite accessible to Westerners.

If you already appreciate Chinese music, try the instrumental anthology *Phases of the Moon: Traditional Chinese Music,* which features a number of traditional instruments not used in the West. Another excellent instrumental choice is *Masterpieces of Chinese Traditional Music.* These offer a wide variety of moods from exuberant to melancholy.

Food

In such a vast and traditionally poor country, it is not surprising that food has a tremendous importance. According to Chinese tradition, food is the bridge between humans and the gods. Humans give the gods food to express their love, and in turn the gods ensure that the people continue to have the good fortune that allows them not to be hungry.

Great Chinese cookbooks abound. Here are a few of my favorites: *Chinese Kitchens* by Eileen Yin-Fei Lo, which includes the history and folklore of the hundreds of dishes featured and a color insert showing a variety of Chinese cooking techniques. If you want less greasy fare, a great choice is *The Chinese Way: Healthy Low-Fat Cooking from China's Regions,* also by Eileen Yin-Fei Lo. Here she gives low-fat recipes for all the standard dishes Americans have come to love—egg rolls, spare ribs, and others. *China the Beautiful Cookbook* by Kevin Sinclair is another cookbook that offers very authentic dishes from throughout China in a lavishly illustrated format.

The meal presented here includes a soup, a main course, a noodle dish, and a vegetable dish. Round out with potstickers (good ones are available in the frozen food section of your grocery store), and don't forget almond or fortune cookies for dessert. If you have trouble getting the ingredients you need for Chinese cooking, check out *www.ethnicgrocer.com.* It features food items and recipes from around the world.

Hot and Sour Soup

I love this soup above all others. There are literally hundreds of ways to prepare it. This recipe is simple and delicious. Add more or less vinegar, sugar, pepper, and soy sauce to get just the taste you want.

½ cup boiling water

½ oz. dried shiitake mushrooms

5 cups chicken stock

⅓ lb. boneless chicken breasts, cut into thin strips

2 teaspoons cornstarch

¼ lb. firm tofu, finely diced

2 tablespoons rice wine vinegar, approximately

2 tablespoons soy sauce, approximately

1 teaspoon sugar

½ teaspoon ground black pepper

In a small bowl, pour the boiling water over the mushrooms, cover and let sit for 15 minutes, until softened. Drain the mushrooms, wash well, and cut into thin strips, discarding hard stems.

In a large saucepan, bring the stock to a boil. Add the chicken and the mushrooms. After it returns to a boil, lower heat and simmer for 10 minutes, covered.

In a small bowl, combine cornstarch with a bit of cold water until smooth. Add the cornstarch mixture and the tofu to the soup, stirring until soup thickens, about 2 minutes. Add the vinegar, soy sauce, sugar, and pepper, and simmer until flavors blend, about 2 minutes. Taste and adjust seasonings to make as hot and sour as you want. Serves 6.

Make Mine Tea

No Chinese meal would be complete without tea. Tea trees are native to China, and tea was first discovered in China in 3000 B.C.E., when some tea leaves accidentally fell into a pot of boiling water in the court of Emperor Shen Nung and the fragrance tempted him to taste it. The cultivation of tea didn't take off, though, until the eighth century, and now there are literally hundreds (some say thousands) of kinds of Chinese tea. They fall into three categories: green (unfermented), oolong (semi-fermented), and black (fully fermented, sometimes called red). A few, slightly fermented, are considered white. For your weekend, be adventurous and try a kind you've never tasted before. Here are some names to try: Dragon Well, the premier green tea said to stimulate the appetite; Iron Goddess, a strong oolong thought to aid digestion; Keemun, the most famous black tea, with a slightly sweet taste; and Silver Needles, a white tea with a faint taste that goes best with vegetables.

If you want to learn a lot more about tea while "in" China, pick up Kit Chow's fascinating book, *All the Tea in China,* a comprehensive look at this delectable topic.

Tangerine Beef

This is a modern twist on a classic Northern Chinese dish. Great over rice or fresh Chinese noodles. You can find the citrus peel at a Chinese market.

2 strips dried citrus fruit peel

4 tablespoons soy sauce

1 tablespoon rice wine vinegar

1 tablespoon cornstarch

2 teaspoons sugar

1 16-oz. steak, sliced into thin strips across the grain

3 tablespoons peanut oil

1 large onion, sliced

1 cup beef stock

2 tablespoons dry sherry

4 small tangerines, peeled and segmented, with juice

1 serrano chili, seeded and finely diced

Soak the citrus peel in hot water for ½ hour or until softened. Drain and finely dice. Combine 2 tablespoons soy sauce, the rice wine vinegar, cornstarch, and 1 teaspoon sugar in a container large enough to hold the steak. Mix well. Add the citrus peel and the steak. Turn to coat steak completely, and allow to sit out for 20 minutes.

Heat a large frying pan or wok until very hot. Add 1 tablespoon of the oil. When it begins to smoke, add half the beef and stir fry until brown, about 3 minutes. With a slotted spoon, remove meat to a plate. Add another tablespoon of oil and stir fry the rest of the beef. Remove to plate.

Put the remaining tablespoon of oil in the pan. Add onions and stir fry until softened. Add the stock, remaining 2 tablespoons soy sauce, sherry, tangerine juice, chili, and remaining teaspoon sugar. Bring to boil, stirring, until liquid is reduced by about half. Return beef to pan, stirring, for 1 minute until heated through. Add the tangerines and stir again. Serves 4.

Ants Climbing Trees

This spicy noodle dish gets its name from its looks—the "trees" are cellophane noodles; the "ants" are the ground pork that cling to the trees. Cellophane noodles are made of mung beans. If you can't find them, you can use regular egg noodles.

8 oz. cellophane noodles

2 tablespoons soy sauce

3 tablespoons peanut oil

2 tablespoons dry sherry

1 teaspoon sesame oil

$\frac{1}{2}$ teaspoon sugar

2 teaspoons chili sauce

8 oz. ground pork

$\frac{3}{4}$ cup chicken broth

Soak the noodles according to package directions. While noodles are soaking, combine 2 tablespoons soy sauce, sherry, 1 tablespoon peanut oil, chili sauce, sesame oil, and sugar in a medium bowl. Add the pork and stir well. Set aside to marinate for $\frac{1}{2}$ hour.

Drain the noodles. Heat a wok or large frying pan until very hot. Add the oil until smoking. Stir fry the pork with marinade until pork is thoroughly cooked, about 3 minutes.

Add the stock, stirring constantly until it begins to boil. Add the noodles and toss until liquid is absorbed. Serves 4.

Spinach with Garlic

2 tablespoons sesame oil

4 garlic cloves, chopped

8 oz. spinach, well washed and drained

2 tablespoons soy sauce

2 tablespoons sesame seeds, toasted
  in toaster oven until roasted

Heat the oil in a wok or frying pan until very hot. Add the garlic and cook until fragrant. Add the spinach and stir fry until wilted, about 2 minutes. Add the soy sauce and sesame seeds. Serves 4.

—M. J. Ryan

Romance and Relaxation in Thailand

WHAT are the images that Thailand brings forth? Ancient cities from past dynasties, monks in saffron-colored robes, monasteries and Buddhist temples, beautiful Thai silk, terracotta pots, carved wooden panels and furniture. Or, the land itself; the bustling metropolis of Bangkok, the mountain villages in the North, and of course the beautiful pristine beaches of the South.

Setting the Scene

Thailand is a land of incredible natural beauty, with tropical rainforests, hot springs, beaches, rice paddies, numerous varieties of flowers, fruit trees, forests of tropical hardwood, and bamboo. And yet, when people who've visited this fabulous country hear the word *Thailand* they first think of the incredible hospitality of the Thai people and the renowned Thai cuisine.

To bring Thailand into your home we are going to create a romantic Thai getaway. Couples from many countries are now traveling to Thailand to escape to paradise, and Thailand has become one of the top honeymoon destinations in the world.

To set the mood for your romantic Thai getaway, you should first create the feeling of being in a tropical rainforest. Bring in large potted plants, such as a yucca, and if you are doing this in the winter, crank up the heat to create a humid, hot atmosphere. Flowers grow in abundance in Thailand—with more than 1,000 varieties of orchids alone. Bring inside or buy orchids, Birds of Paradise, jasmine, or whatever fragrant blooms you can find to create the hot fragrant atmosphere. Bring in a variety of pillows, and if you have any pieces of silk material, drape them over your furniture.

If you have a small fountain, be sure to turn it on so you'll hear the sound of water flowing. Many large chain stores carry small sound machines to help people sleep at night. These machines have settings for the ocean, birds calling, rain falling, or even crickets in the night. For your Thai getaway you can pick the soothing sounds of rain falling in the forest. With the plants and flowers and sounds of the rainforest, you have now created the perfect setting for relaxation and romance.

Buddhism is the predominant religion in Thailand, with every village containing a temple or monastery. In Thai homes, businesses, and hotels, you will see elaborately decorated miniature homes placed in corners. These "spirit houses" are the homes of the resident spirit of the place. Often they are tiny replicas of the Thai house or sometimes elaborately decorated shrines. In front of them you will find small dishes of rice and other foods, and sticks of incense. Keep the spirit happy, and harmony and good fortune will reign. If problems arise, the spirit houses are refurbished and moved, and the spirit is placated with food, flowers, incense, candles, and other offerings.

So, for your Thai getaway, you may want to create your own personal altar space. On a mantel, bookshelf, or low table, place objects or pictures that hold special significance for you or your partner. Two good resources offering instruction and inspiration for creating personal altars are *Altars and Icons: Sacred Spaces in Everyday Life* by Jean McMann and *Sacred Space:*

Clearing and Enhancing the Energy of Your Home by Denise Linn.

For your dress I would suggest putting on a sarong and going barefoot. In Thailand, this is the standard dress of both men and women. If you do decide to have a weekend with just your sweetie, one great thing to do together is to give each other Thai massages. If you are doing this weekend during hot weather and live near a beach, be sure to include a bit of sun and sand, for Thailand is loaded with beautiful beaches. And if you can find a secluded spot, that will only add to the romance.

*B*ooks

Look up these beautiful photography books to help you in setting the perfect Thai scene. *Tropical Asian Style* by Luca Invenizzi Tettoni is a gorgeous, colorful collection of homes throughout Southeast Asia. Notice how the architecture and interiors of the houses blend so beautifully into their surroundings. You'll quickly be ready to redecorate your home with teak furniture and Thai silk. Similarly, *Thai Style* by William Warren depicts the architecture, furnishings, and gardens of many places throughout Thailand. This book is also a wonderful re-

Massage Thai-Style

Thai massage is a unique form of bodywork dating back to ancient times that was developed by monks who sat in meditation for long periods of time. Incorporating elements of gentle rocking, deep stretching, and rhythmic compression, Thai massage will revitalize your body and mind. Deeply therapeutic, it benefits both the giver and receiver. Two excellent resources are *Thai Massage: A Traditional Medical Technique* by Dr. Richard Gold and *Thai Massage Manual: Natural Therapy for Flexibility, Relaxation and Energy Balance* by Maria Mercati.

source for Thai history, arts, and crafts. William Warren's other book, *Thailand: The Golden Kingdom,* is a wonderful overview of the diversity and beauty of Thailand—from the beaches of the South to the mountains of the North.

You may find little time for reading on your Thai getaway, but if you would like to read some novels in your research there are one or two books worth mentioning. *The English Governess at the Siamese Court* by Anna Harriette Leonowens is the famous memoir of Leonowens' time teaching the children of the King of Siam. Originally published in 1870, this fascinating account of nineteenth-century Siam has been made into two movies, *The King and I* (the 1956 classic with Yul Brynner and Deborah Kerr) and *Anna and the King* (the 1999 version with Jodie Foster and Chow Yun-Fat), as well as a famous Rodgers and Hammerstein musical.

Before *The Beach* made headlines as Leonardo DiCaprio's follow-up movie to *Titanic,* it was making headlines as the novel by Alex Garland. In it Garland's hero searches and finds the perfect paradise off the coast of Southern Thailand. This is a gripping suspense tale that speaks to the yearning we all have to find the ultimate Eden (and the human tendency to ultimately pollute and destroy these places, à la *Lord of the Flies).*

Videos

Two beautiful travel videos will help in setting the scene for your escape to Thailand. *The Living Edens: Thailand: Jewel of the Orient* has soft hypnotic music flowing in the background as scenes of ancient Buddhist temples, lush tropical forests, and the many different animals of the region appear onscreen. For a look at the cities, towns, and countryside of Thailand, and great insight into Thai food, watch *Land of Smiles: Thailand.* These videos and more can all be found on Amazon.com.

If it is video entertainment you seek, check out *The Beach* or one of the versions of *The King and I.*

*M*usic

Like the music of other countries, music from Thailand presents listeners with a vast array of choices depending on taste—modern rock, classical, folk, or music from any of the different regions of the country.

For modern Thai pop and rock, check out the Web sites *Thaicdnow.com* and *sawutdee.net. Ancient-Contemporary Music from Thailand* by Fong Naam blends classical Thai instruments with electronic sounds. *Thailande-Thailand: Ko Samui,* a collection by Air Mail Music is a compilation of the type of Thai music you would expect to hear in villages and temples, while *Classical Music of Northern Thailand,* performed by the Lanna Orchid Ensemble of Chiang Mai University, uses the northern instruments of the *salaw* (free bow fiddle), *saw* (single-reed pipe), and *seung* (plucked lute).

Food

Internationally famous, Thai food is a tasty combination of sweet, sour, hot, and salty flavors that combine to create an unforgettable dining experience. Thai cooking actually blends together a variety of ancient traditions into a unique whole. Traditionally, the Thai cooking methods of stewing, baking, or grilling have been combined with Chinese influences of frying and stir-frying. In the 1600s Portuguese missionaries introduced the chilies they had found in South America to Thailand. These pairings, combined with the influences of Dutch, French, and Japanese traditions, have all helped create the Thai food we appreciate today.

There are literally hundred of cookbooks on Thai cooking. *Cracking the Coconut: Classic Thai Home Cooking* by Su-Mei Yu provides hundreds of mouth-watering recipes and detailed instructions on how to make chili pastes, fresh coconut milk, and a variety of other key ingredients. *Real Thai: The Best of Thailand's Regional Cooking* by Nancie McDermott is organized geographically by region and includes advice on basic utensils and techniques, a glossary of ingredients, a list of shopping sources, and a section of suggested menus. *Simply Thai Cooking* by Wandee Young has easy-to-follow recipes for all of the traditional dishes. A favorite, *True Thai: The Modern Art of Thai Cooking* by Victor Sodsook has more than 230 recipes from cities and countryside throughout Thailand. A wonderful resource is the chapter on fruit and vegetable carving in the back. With Victor's help you can make sure the food presentation will be as wonderful as the food itself.

Once you are ready to start the meal, decorate your table with lots of flowers, prepare the jasmine rice (the fragrant rice of Thai cooking, available at most supermarkets), and get ready to feast. Served all at once, a proper Thai meal should consist of a soup, a curry dish, and a dip with fish and vegetables. Spring rolls and *satay* can be served as further side dishes or as a snack. For our Thai meal we will be serving vegetarian spring rolls, chicken-coconut soup, yellow curry with chicken, sweet and sour vegetables, and to finish off, fresh oranges and flower petals. Any unusual ingredients can be found at Asian markets or online at *ethnicgrocer.com*.

Thai Vegetarian Spring Rolls

1 16 oz pkg. dried bean vermicelli noodles

2 carrots, grated

4 scallions, finely sliced

1 stalk celery, finely diced

10 cloves garlic, finely sliced

½ cup fresh cilantro including stems, loosely chopped

1 8 oz can bamboo shoots, sliced

5 tablespoons soy sauce

5 tablespoons sugar

1 teaspoon black pepper

1 pkg. spring roll wrappers

peanut oil for deep-frying

Dipping Sauce

½ cup white vinegar

1 cup sugar

½ teaspoon salt

1 clove crushed garlic

1 teaspoon Thai chili sauce, or to taste

Soak the noodles for 12–15 minutes in a large bowl of warm water. As the noodles become soft and pliable, spread them in the bowl for even soaking. Drain the noodles in a colander and lay them out on a cutting board. Cut the noodles into quarters.

Place the noodles, carrots, scallions, celery, garlic, cilantro, and bamboo shoots into a large mixing bowl. Mix well with your hands, and then add the soy sauce, sugar, and pepper. Toss together.

Heat a large wok or skillet to medium-high and stir fry the noodle mixture until the vegetables become moist and the noodles soft and clear (about 4 minutes). Transfer the filling back to the large bowl and allow to cool.

Gently separate the spring roll wrappers from the pack. Place two wrappers one on top of the other, to create a double thickness, on a flat surface with a pointed edge toward you. Keep the rest of the wrappers covered with a damp paper towel. Place about 3 tablespoons of the filling in the center of the wrappers. Fold the bottom of the wrapper up and over the filling, tucking it under the filling to form a cylinder. Fold the right and left sides in toward the middle, then roll it tightly right up to the top. Moisten the edges with water to seal the roll. Set the roll on a platter with the seam side down. Continue making the spring rolls until you have used up the filling.

To make the dipping sauce, combine the vinegar and 1/2 cup of the sugar in a small saucepan. Bring to a low boil, stirring occasionally. Reduce the heat to medium and stir in the rest of the sugar. Cook for 2 minutes, stirring frequently as the mixture comes to a boil. Reduce the heat to low and add the salt and garlic. Simmer for 5 minutes, stirring occasionally. Stir in the chili sauce and remove from heat. Cool to room temperature.

When you are ready to eat, pour the peanut oil into a large wok or skillet and heat the oil until sizzling hot. Put a spring roll in the hot oil. It should sizzle immediately. Add a couple more and fry, turning them occasionally, 3 minutes or until they are golden brown. Remove the spring rolls with a wire skimmer or spoon, and drain them on a plate lined with paper towels. Cut the spring rolls and serve with dipping sauce. Serves 6.

Tom Kha Gai

CHICKEN-COCONUT SOUP

The chili-tamarind paste for this recipe is available at Asian markets.

1 large stalk lemongrass
3 cups chicken stock or canned
    chicken broth
10 slices unpeeled ginger
peel of 1 lime
½ lb. mushrooms, sliced
2 14 oz cans coconut milk (may be
    low-fat version)

½ pound boneless chicken breast,
    cut up into bite-sized pieces
2 tablespoons chili-tamarind paste
⅓ cup fresh lemon juice
3 tablespoons sugar
2½ tablespoons fish sauce
6 small chilies (optional)

Half of a
coconut

Discard the tough outer leaves of the lemongrass and cut into 2-inch pieces. Put the chicken stock, ginger, lemongrass, and lime peel into a large soup pot. Gradually bring to boil over medium-high heat. Boil for 1 minute, then stir in the mushrooms, coconut milk, and chicken, and return the mixture to boil. Add in the chili-tamarind paste, lemon juice, sugar, and fish sauce. Stir until the chili-tamarind paste and sugar are dissolved. For extra spice you can garnish the soup with the chilies. Discard the ginger, lemongrass stalks, and lime. Peel before serving. Serves 4.

Gaeng Garee Gai

YELLOW CURRY WITH CHICKEN

Curry Paste

1 piece ginger, peeled and chopped

2 tablespoons chopped lemongrass

1 teaspoon salt

4 cloves crushed garlic

1 teaspoon shrimp paste

¼ teaspoon cayenne pepper

Sauce

5 tablespoons corn syrup

1 tablespoon vinegar

⅓ cup cucumber, peeled and thinly sliced

12 ground roasted peanuts

few slices chili pepper

Chicken

2 cups coconut milk

1 teaspoon curry powder

½ lb. chicken breast, thinly sliced

3 small potatoes, peeled and cut
   into small pieces

2 tablespoons sugar

2 tablespoons soy sauce

Begin by making the curry paste. Combine the ginger, lemongrass, salt, garlic, shrimp paste, and cayenne pepper together. Liquidize in a food processor or blender for about 10 seconds or until paste is smooth.

To make the sauce, simply mix the corn syrup, vinegar, cucumber, and peanuts together.

In a saucepan bring the coconut milk to a boil. Mix in the curry paste and the curry powder. Cook for 2 minutes, then add the chicken pieces and potato. Stir together and add the sugar and soy sauce. Simmer for about 10 minutes until the chicken and potato are cooked. Serve with sauce and jasmine rice. Serves 4.

Phad Priawan Phak

SWEET AND SOUR VEGETABLES

Sauce

2 tablespoons lime juice

2 tablespoons sugar

1 tablespoon fish sauce

1 tablespoon oyster sauce

2 tablespoons soy sauce

5 tablespoons tomato sauce

Vegetables

4 tablespoons vegetable oil

3 cloves crushed garlic

1 onion, sliced

1 small head broccoli, cut into
   bite-sized pieces

1 medium carrot, peeled and cut
   into 1-inch pieces

2 small zucchini, cut into 1-inch strips

1 cucumber, peeled and cut into 1-inch pieces

$\frac{1}{2}$ cup pineapple, cut into bite-sized pieces

1 chili pepper, cut into thin strips

2 tomatoes, chopped

1 cup snow peas

$\frac{1}{2}$ cup sliced mushrooms

To make the sauce, combine the lime juice, sugar, fish sauce, oyster sauce, soy sauce, and tomato sauce together. Set aside.

Heat a wok up with the oil and fry the garlic until it is golden brown. Add the onion and stir fry until tender, about 3 minutes. Add the broccoli, carrot, and zucchini, followed by cucumber and pineapple; stir fry for 2 minutes after each addition. Add the chilies, tomatoes, peas, and mushrooms and stir fry until all the vegetables are cooked. Add the sauce at the very end, toss together, and serve. Serves 4.

Fresh Oranges and Flower Petals

4 navel oranges	Crushed ice
2 cups water	Fresh nasturtium flower petals
1 cup sugar	

Peel the oranges, removing the pits and skin. Divide into segments, then place the orange segments in a glass bowl, cover, and refrigerate.

In a saucepan combine the water and sugar and bring to a boil, until the sugar is dissolved. Continue to boil gently (about 15 minutes) until the mixture becomes syrupy. Remove and let cool and room temperature before chilling.

When you are ready to serve, arrange the orange slices on a dish. Pour on the syrup and add several handfuls of crushed ice. Garnish with the fresh flower petals and serve. Serves 4.

—Heather McArthur

For the Truly Adventurous

A Thai delicacy, *durian* fruit can be found at many Asian markets. This large, irregular shaped fruit with its thick spiky shell is known for not only its rich butter-almond taste, but for the incredibly bad smell it emits. In fact, the smell is so bad that it is banned from most hotels and restaurants. But folks swear by the fruit's great taste.

Journey to Japan

TRYING to capture the essence of a culture that is deep and rich from an uninterrupted 2,000 years of development is in many ways difficult. On the other hand, the options for an armchair weekend are incredible. Somewhere within the traditions of the samurai, geisha houses, Zen Buddhism, Pokeman, Pachinko, and Japanese animation, there is a theme for just about every

Setting the Scene

occasion. You could dress up in a kimono, sit on the floor and serve meals on the coffee table, and recreate the atmosphere of feudal Japan, or you could have people show up as their favorite cultural icon, be it Godzilla, Pokeman, or Princess Monomoke, and have a Japanese film fest.

There is also a wealth of inexpensive items available in Japanese import stores to help set the scene. Beautifully decorated cotton prints can be hung in doorways or on the wall; colorful *yukatas* (a cotton kimono-like garment) and an assortment of small classically designed bowls and plates and sake containers will not only help to set the stage but will be useful during the meal.

If you are going the classic route, you can pick up a couple of thin beach mats that are woven out of rice stalks and give the illusion of the ever-present tatami mats of historic Japan. It would help to have some incense burning and maybe a small artfully done shrine with photos of your ancestors tucked neatly in a private corner of a room.

At some point during the weekend, consider pulling out some rice paper, ink, and brushes for a foray into Japanese brush stroke painting, calligraphy, or haiku.

If you want to speak a bit of Japanese, it's pretty easy. Most words in Japanese are combinations of simple two- or three-letter syllables. *Hai* (pronounced "hi") means "Yes," *Ii* ("Ee-yay") means "No," *gomen* ("go-men") is "I'm sorry," *ohayou* ("o-hi-o") is "Good morning," *konnichiwa* ("ko-nee-chi-wa") is "Good afternoon." When listening to someone else, nod your head to everything they say and mutter *So desu ne* ("so des nay") over

and over again. Far and away the most spoken phrase in Japanese, it is loosely translated as "Yes, that's true!"

Books ....

Following is an eclectic mix of the breadth rather than depth of Japanese literature.
 If you want a coffee-table book, there are hundreds, with exquisite photos centered on themes from the costumes and mask of Japanese theatre

Haiku

The shortest of all literary forms and native to Japan, haiku traditionally consists of three lines of seventeen syllables usually distributed in three lines of five, seven, and five syllables. Haiku is meant to capture a moment or surprise about nature. An example by the late seventeenth-century master Basho:

> *Weathered bones*
> *just thinking of the wind*
> *it pierces my body*

and the armor and helmets made for the samurai to the more standard scenic tours of Japan's hot spots and neon glitter of the big cities. A good place to start is *Images of Japan: Japan the Four Seasons* by Johnny Hymas.

In the serious reading genre, you can always start at the beginning with *The Tale of Genji,* by Murasaki Shikibu, which is widely considered to be the world's first true novel. Even here, Japan is never simple, as there is a heated controversy over which translation is better: Edward Seidensticker's (considered easier to follow and more literal a translation) or Arthur Waley's (which strives to put some of the poetry lost in translation back into the story).

If there is a modern "standard" of the Japanese literary canon, it would have to be *Confessions of a Mask* by Yukio Mishima. Nothing about Mishima, from his homosexuality and brilliant literary career to his militaristic nationalism and spectacularly-staged suicide, is straightforward, and yet he stands as a lasting icon of modern-day Japan. If *Confessions of a Mask* is too much to wade through in a weekend, *The Sailor Who Fell from Grace with the Sea* is much more accessible, if just as disturbing.

The lead story from *The Izu Dancer and Other Stories* is a wonderful choice for reading aloud. It is by Japan's first Nobel Prize-winning author and a contemporary of Mishima, Yasunari Kawabata. First published in 1925, *The Izu Dancer* is an autobiographical account of Kawabata's unrequited romance with a young dancer. Two of Kawabata's best-known novels are *Snow Country* and *The Sound of the Mountains.*

Kenzaburo Oe is Japan's second Nobel Prize-winner, and his work stands as a highlight of Japan's complexity. In a country that has an almost pathological drive to avoid emotion, *A Personal Matter,* Oe's most famous novel, is an emotionally gripping, semi-autobiographical account of the struggle to deal with the birth of a severely mentally handicapped son. In a culture where fathers have almost no role in raising children, Oe's close relationship to his son is a theme that runs in one way or another throughout his entire body of work. In fact, right after accepting the Nobel Prize in 1994, Oe announced that his career as a writer was over since his writing had been to give voice to his son, and by then his son, Hikari Oe, had become an established composer with his own voice.

In the new, noteworthy, and perhaps more generally accessible category is Kiyohiro Miura's novel about his young son's attraction to Zen and eventual ordination as a priest at age thirteen, *He's Leaving Home: My*

Young Son Becomes a Zen Monk. And if you want to sink into a long, entertaining tale, don't overlook the wildly popular inside look at the world of the geisha, Arthur S. Golden's *Memoirs of a Geisha.*

Videos

Next to Hollywood, Japan is one of the richest and broadest centers of film in the world. My personal list starts with *Tokyo Story* (1953). It is a simple story of an elderly couple who travel to Tokyo to visit their children and find indifference, irritation, and selfishness. Thought to be Yasujiro Ozu's finest work and considered by many to be one of the most perfect films ever made, *Tokyo Story* is the ultimate meditation on mortality.

For an immersion in the contradictions of modern Japan, see *Mishima: A Life in Four Chapters* (1995) directed by Paul Schrader. It's a fascinating film that manages to reflect within its own structure, acting, cinematography, and soundtrack much of the deep complexity of Mishima's life.

In my opinion, Akira Kurosawa was the creator of some of the most visually stunning films ever made. My three top choices are *Rashomon* (1950), *Kagemusha* (1980), and *Ran*

(1985). *Rashomon* is a rendering of a brutal crime as told by different characters. Interestingly, the stories were written by Ryunosuke Akutagawa, after whom the most prestigious Japanese film award (often won by Kurosawa) is named. *Kagemusha (The Shadow Warrior)* has for my money the most extraordinarily beautiful opening scene in cinema, while *Ran,* Kurosawa's version of King Lear, is so finely done, so exquisitely beautiful, and so flawlessly shot and edited (Kurosawa hand-painted virtually every scene in the movie before beginning filming) that the bard himself would be speechless.

I also strongly suggest *Woman in the Dunes* (1964) directed by Hiroshi Teshigahara. You'll either love this black-and-white film and it will stick in your mind forever, or you'll hate it. Either way, it's an unforgettable experience.

On a lighter note, consider the king of monster movies, *Gojira* (1954), directed by Ishiro Honda. This is the original subtitled Godzilla movie, and the Americanized version that came out a year later with Raymond Burr edited in as a reporter is almost as good.

If you want a fine example of Japanese animation, look at *Princess Mononoke* (1999), the all-time box office leader in Japan, directed by Hayao Miyazaki, the master of Japanese animation.

Finally, for a mix of ancient roots and Western veneer, pick up *The Pillow Book* (1996), directed by Peter Greenaway. This luscious, sensual film has developed a very devoted following among Japanese college students and is well worth viewing—without children.

Music

Like much Eastern music, traditional Japanese music can be an acquired taste for Westerners. If you want to dive in, a great introduction is *Japan: Traditional Vocal and Instrumental Music* recorded by the Ensemble Nipponia in the late '80s. It's an excellent introduction with pieces drawn from both court music and theater. A little more accessible is *Japan: Shakuhachi—The Japanese Flute,* a collection of different artists' rendering of traditional wooden flute pieces.

If you are adventuresome enough to explore Japanese folk music, *Min'yo: Folk Songs from Japan* by Takahashi Yujiro is an excellent collection. Even more accessible is a wonderful collection of Japanese traditional melodies performed by Irish flautist James Galaway, *The Enchanted Forest-Melodies of Japan.* The Western flute and synthesizer bring a degree of familiarity that makes it easier on the untrained ear and yet it is still beautifully true to the traditional character of the music.

If you are reading something by Kenzaburo Oe, you might want to complete the picture by getting *Music of Hikari Oe.* It is a hauntingly beautiful album of original classical compositions and the "voice" that prompted his father to give up writing.

Finally, the modern music scene in Japan is extremely vital and varied. The best sampler I could find, which gives you a taste of the range of popular music being produced in Japan today, is the *Rough Guide: The Music of Japan,* which offers everything from Okinawa-pop and taiko-rap to avant-garde instrumentals.

Food

Japan has the most unique of the great cuisines in the world. Like all great cooking traditions, available natural resources formed the essential character of Japanese cooking. In this sharply mountainous collection of islands, there were an extremely limited amount of agricultural space, which put a premium on meats of any kind, and a bounty of food available from the surrounding sea. It's no accident that sushi has become the signature food of Japan.

If you want the perfect Japanese meal, you should eat *Kaiseki* style. That is a meal where one small delicately prepared dish after another appears in front of you. In a good restaurant the meal can go on for hours, and every dish is unique and exquisite.

There are plenty of delicious alternatives. Most Japanese meals have at least a handful of small side dishes, so we'll start there (ingredients should be readily available at Asian markets). We then go onto two well-known and delicious main courses. Desserts are not really a tradition in Japan, so I suggest finishing the meal off with a chilled glass of plum wine.

You will need a set of small dishes, bowls, chopsticks (the Japanese word is *hashi* ["ha she"]). Hashi are shorter, tapered chopsticks; Chinese chopsticks are longer and cylindrical. You can usually find these at almost any import store, where you'll find plenty of other mood-setting as well as practical Japanese items such as fabrics and a few good cushions to sit on while you eat.

Recipes abound for many fabulous dishes. Some of my favorites are *Oyako donburi* or *Katsu donburi*, which is a mix of chicken or pork with egg and onion in a sauce that is poured on top a bowl of steaming rice. Another favorite, not nearly as well known in the West, is *Okonomiyaki,* a big pancake with all kinds of great things in it.

A good, simple-to-follow cookbook is *The Essentials of Japanese Cooking* by Tokiko Suzuki; a little more sophisticated is *The Japanese Kitchen: 250 Recipes in a Traditional Spirit* by Ming Tsai. For those of you who get really hooked, *The Folk Art of Japanese Country Cooking: A Traditional Diet for Today's World* by Gaku Homma is as much a history and exploration of how Japanese country cooking developed as it is a great cookbook.

Spinach Salad with Sesame Seeds

water
salt to taste
1 large bunch spinach
1 tablespoon soy sauce

2 teaspoons sake
2 tablespoons sesame seeds, lightly ground

Set out a large bowl of ice water and bring a pan of lightly salted water to boil on the stove. After rinsing the spinach, toss two or three leaves at a time into the boiling water for 2 minutes and then immerse immediately in the ice water. Repeat until all the spinach is cooked. Squeeze lightly to drain and then cut into inch-long pieces. Mix gently with the soy sauce and sake and sprinkle with the sesame. Serves 4.

Hijiki

Dashi is one of the central ingredients in Japanese cooking. It is essentially a fish broth made from bonita and konbu seaweed. You can get the ingredients to make it from scratch in many Asian markets, but instant dashi is plenty good enough.

1 handful dried hijiki seaweed	4 tablespoons soy sauce
1 carrot, washed and scraped	4 tablespoons sake
1 teaspoon vegetable oil	2 cups dashi

Soak the hijiki in hot water until soft then boil for 1 minute. Mince the carrot. Heat the oil in a frying pan and stir fry the carrot for about 5 minutes; then add the soy sauce, sake, and hijiki and fry for a few more minutes. To blend the flavors. Add the dashi, cover and boil for 5 minutes, then simmer uncovered until there is just a little sauce left in the pan (about 10 minutes). Serve warm or cold. Serves 4.

Daikon Pickle

Daikon is a big, white Japanese radish that looks like a giant white carrot, and *konbu* is a thick and wide piece of seaweed that is used to flavor many Japanese dishes.

⅓ daikon radish	1 tablespoon thinly sliced lime peel
1 small piece of konbu	soy sauce to cover

Peel the daikon and cut into pieces about ¼ by ½ inches. Cut the konbu into a few pieces. Put the daikon, lime peel, and konbu into a container and add soy sauce to about three-quarters of an inch high. Cover, shake, and leave overnight. Serves 4.

Miso Soup

There are hundreds of variations of this classic, with ingredients such as cabbage, green onions, mushrooms, onions, leeks, squash, snow peas, green beans, bean sprouts, and even thin slices of potato. In buying miso paste, be aware that *aka-miso* (red miso) is the stronger and more salty one, and *shiro-miso* (white miso) is milder. Here is a basic, great recipe.

4 cups dashi	4 tablespoons miso paste
½ lb. tofu cut into ½-inch cubes	2 green onions, chopped
4 fresh shiitake mushrooms, sliced thin	

Boil the dashi, add the tofu and mushrooms, and simmer for 4 minutes. Add the miso and turn off the stove as soon as it is completely dissolved. Toss in the green onion and serve. Serves 4.

Sukiyaki

Sukiyaki is an interactive meal best made at the table in an electric wok or with a portable burner. It is a soupy concoction in which the meat, noodles, and vegetables float. *Shirataki* noodles are made from a kind of yam and are found either packed in liquid in the refrigerated section of the store or canned.

2 cups short grain rice	soy sauce
4 eggs	1 onion, sliced
cooking oil, as needed	10 stalks green onion, chopped 1-inch long

1 1b. thinly sliced beef

dashi

sake

sugar

6 fresh shiitake mushrooms, sliced

2 pkgs. fresh shirataki noodles
(about a half-pound each)

Steam the rice, preferably in a rice cooker. Then prepare the table with chopsticks, a bowl for rice, and four small bowls each with a raw beaten egg inside.

Heat the wok. Add some oil and some slices of beef. Then add $\frac{1}{4}$ cup dashi, a splash of sake, a teaspoon of soy sauce, and $\frac{1}{2}$ teaspoon of sugar to start. Adjust the amount as you add more according to your own preference. Don't worry, you'll get the hang of it quickly.

Add a handful of each of the rest of the ingredients and cook till tender, stirring with long chopsticks. When done, remove with chopsticks and dip directly in the bowl with the beaten egg and then eat with the steamed rice. Continue to add ingredients until everyone has had their fill. Serves 4.

Zaru Soba

This is a simple and delicious favorite. *Soba* is a buckwheat noodle that is famous in the North of Japan. *Mirin* is a sweet rice cooking wine, *nori* is the thin sheets of blackish green seaweed you see in sushi, and *wasabe* is a kind of Japanese horseradish that is finely grated into a hot paste. It's not always possible to get fresh wasabe, but you can always find a powdered wasabe that you just add water to.

¾ lb. dry soba noodles

1 1-inch piece of peeled ginger, sliced into matchsticks

1 small carrot, peeled and sliced into matchsticks

4 green onions, finely chopped

2 cups dashi

½ cup soy sauce

½ cup mirin

1 sheet nori, sliced into very thin strips

Small amount of wasabe

Bring pot of water to boil and add the soba noodles. When water begins to boil again add 1 cup of cold water, bring back to a boil and boil until noodles are tender (about 3 minutes). Drain the noodles and run under cold water, drain and set aside.

Blanch the ginger, carrot, and green onion in a small pot of boiling water for around 30 seconds, then drain and cool in a small bowl of ice water. Drain and set aside.

Make the sauce by combining the dashi, soy sauce, and mirin in a small pot. Boil for 1 minute, then allow to cool.

To serve, divide the cold soba noodles onto four serving platters, the vegetables into four small bowls, the dipping sauce into four bowls, and the nori and wasabe on a small serving platter for each place. Take a little of the noodles, nori, and wasabe at a time, dip in the sauce, and make sure you slurp really loudly as you eat. Serves 4.

— *Will Glennon*

Some Like It Hot

Sake was discovered in the third century and quickly became a central part of the Japanese diet. Like most alcoholic beverages around the world, the making of sake rapidly became an art form, engendering passionate arguments about what is the best sake and the best way to make sake.

In its original form, there are only three ingredients in sake—rice, water, and the magic mold *koji*. During WWII, with shortages everywhere, brewers' alcohol was added to boost production and incidentally set off an argument that is still debated. The "purists" insist that the best sake has no added alcohol, while many very respected sake critics claim that a small amount of added alcohol actually brings out the flavors better.

In all sake the rice is milled to some degree before brewing, and the degree of milling is a key factor in the end result. The four major types of sake are *Junmai-shu*, which contains no added alcohol and where at most 70 percent of the grain is left after the rice has been milled. It tends to be a bit heavy. *Honjozo-shu* has a small amount of ethyl alcohol added and also must use rice with at least 30 percent of the grain milled off. With *Ginjo-shu* you begin to get into top-quality sake. It starts with rice milled so that no more than 60 percent of the grain remains and involves a much more labor-intensive fermentation process. Finally, at the top of the quality ladder, there is *Daiginjo-shu*, which begins with no more than 50 percent of the grain remaining.

The American image of sake is that you drink it hot, but that is really not a good idea unless the sake is very cheap. Most sake should be drunk either chilled, like a Chardonnay, or at room temperature, like a good red wine.

Idling in Australia

LOTS of North Americans fantasize about visiting Australia. With a lifestyle in many ways not dissimilar to ours, what is it exactly about Aussie Land that so captures people's imaginations? Perhaps the abundance of long beautiful beaches; the wildlife (who can resist the idea of seeing kangaroos bounding across the outback?); the *frisson* of knowing that many of the world's most poisonous varieties of snakes and spiders are Australian, as are those notoriously ferocious saltwater crocodiles; or the thought of endless blue skies and clear, piercing sunlight. With an area as big as the lower forty-eight of the United States, Australia encompasses many climates and landscapes, from the red soil desert

Setting the Scene

of the interior to the tropical rainforests of Queensland, so perhaps it's just the range of possibilities.

To get in the mood, find some lavish picture books of Australian scenery, and lay them open invitingly on a table ready to leaf through. Put up some posters of beaches, or koalas, or the striking monolithic Uluru (Ayers Rock) glowing red at sunset, or the famous white sails of the Sydney Opera House roofline against a blue sky, or a sweet-faced mother 'roo with her baby joey peeking out of her pouch. (You could cheat if you can't find posters, and go to your local travel agent and look for their glossy brochures on tours to Australia, which will almost certainly feature some of those things on the covers, and put them up instead!) If you've already visited Australia, now's the time to drag out all of your souvenirs. Put the eucalyptus hand soap out in the bathroom, the sheepskin rug in front of the hearth, and the aboriginal print up on the wall. If

KNOWN AS THE **TREE BEAR** BY THE AUSTRALIAN COLONISTS BUT IT IS NOT A BEAR
KNOWN AS THE **WOMBAT** BY THE AMERICAN FURRIER BUT IT IS NOT A WOMBAT

you happen to have an old surfboard gathering dust in the garage, bring it in and prop it up in the living room.

What else should you do? Settle in and watch some fine Australian movies. Or if you're so inclined, get out a deck of cards, and put some money on a game. Better yet, if there's a possibility for off-track betting where you live, study the racing form section of the newspaper, and play the ponies... Australians are notorious for their love of gambling. (Some say that they'll bet on two flies crawling up a wall.)

If you're a sports fan, check the television listings to see if any cricket or Aussie-rules football is being shown. Aussie rules is a fast-paced and exciting game, said to be a mix of rugby and soccer, where the players, without an ounce of padding or protection, sometimes collide so hard that it'll make you wince. If you're lucky you'll catch the incongruous sight of big, lunky football players taking high balletic leaps into the air for the ball. Cricket, in contrast, may seem slow and possibly incomprehensible, but it's a cousin of baseball, so stick with it for a few minutes and you'll get the hang of it. It's worth a look just to hear the announcer, usually with calm, almost reverent voice, refer to the locations of the players on the field as "silly mid-on" or "deep backward square leg."

If you'd prefer something a little gentler, plan to serve a lavish afternoon tea. Like the Brits, Australians love a good cup of tea, accompanied by some sweet baked treats. Scones are the classic, as are lamingtons, an Aussie white cake rolled in chocolate and coconut (there's a recipe in *Australia: The Beautiful Cookbook*). Another way to Aussie-fy your tea would be to make

Waltzing Matilda

Written in 1895 by A. B. "Banjo" Patterson, one of Australia's most famous bush poets, the tune "Waltzing Matilda" is recognized around the world. But outside of Australia few people understand what on earth it's really about. A couple of versions exist with slightly different wording; here's a well-known one:

Once a jolly swagman camped by a billabong,
Under the shade of a coolibah-tree,
And he sang as he watched and waited till his billy boiled,
"Who'll come a-waltzing Matilda with me?
Waltzing Matilda, Waltzing Matilda,
Who'll come a-waltzing Matilda with me?"
And he sang as he watched and waited till his billy boiled,
"Who'll come a-waltzing Matilda with me?"

Down came a jumbuck to drink at the billabong:
Up jumped the swagman and grabbed him with glee.
And he sang as he shoved that jumbuck in his tucker-bag,
"You'll come a-waltzing Matilda with me.
Waltzing Matilda, Waltzing Matilda,
You'll come a-waltzing Matilda with me."
And he sang as he shoved that jumbuck in his tucker-bag,
"You'll come a-waltzing Matilda with me."

Up rode a squatter, mounted on his thoroughbred;
Down came the troopers, one, two, three:
"Who's that jolly jumbuck you've got in your tucker-bag?
You'll come a-waltzing Matilda with me!

Waltzing Matilda, Waltzing Matilda,
You'll come a-waltzing Matilda with me.
Who's that jolly jumbuck you've got in your tucker-bag?
You'll come a-waltzing Matilda with me!"

Up jumped the swagman and sprang into the billabong;
"You'll never catch me alive!" said he;
And his ghost may be heard as you pass by that billabong,
"You'll come a-waltzing Matilda with me!
Waltzing Matilda, Waltzing Matilda,
You'll come a-waltzing Matilda with me!"
And his ghost may be heard as you pass by that billabong,
"You'll come a-waltzing Matilda with me!"

A *swagman* was a hobo, an itinerant, who traveled the countryside carrying his belongings wrapped in a cloth known as a swag. *Billabong* is the aboriginal word for an oxbow lake. The *coolibah* tree is a variety of eucalyptus commonly found beside water. A *billy* is a tin can, usually with a wire handle, in which people in the bush boiled water to make tea. *Jumbuck* is a word, no longer in use, for a sheep. *Tucker* is food, so a *tucker-bag* is a storage bag for same. A *squatter* was a land-holding farmer who achieved this good fortune simply by laying claim to the land when the country was wide open, and envied by others thereafter. *Troopers* were soldiers, or policemen.

The song's title is said to derive from a couple of European expressions. The German *auf der walz* means to travel around the country, earning a living as you go. And *Matilda* is a term that transmuted from a female camp follower in times of war, to someone who keeps you warm at night, and eventually came to describe the troops' greatcoats or blankets. Put the two together, and you have someone who travels around carrying a blanket. So now that you know, try singing it!

some passion fruit curd (see sidebar in Food section). Then heap the curd onto your scones, just as you would lemon curd.

Australians dress casually almost all of the time, so if weather permits, put on your shorts and flip flops to look like a native. Some people really do greet each other with "G'day, mate," so practice saying that 'til you've got the accent right. And should anyone ask anything of you, your response should be "No worries" or "Not a problem," as life in Australia is always relaxed.

And the most important thing of all, lay in a good supply of Fosters, Australia's best-loved beer, for the weekend! It's not an authentic Australian experience without the Fosters, so drink it early and often.

*B*ooks

Having suggested that you display some photo books, I'll start with those. *Australian Colors: Images of the Outback* has gorgeous photographs by Bill Bachman, and, as a bonus, essays by Tim Winton, a terrific Aussie writer. Ken Duncan is famous throughout Australia for his wide-format landscape photography, mainly taken in the country and the outback. *Australia Wide: A Panoramic View* is my favorite of his, although you may find the more recently published *The Great South Land* easier to come by.

Spectacular Australia by Phillip Matthews has images by a number of photographers; to my mind some of the most interesting pictures are the aerials taken in the outback, as they allow you an unusual perspective on the patterns in land formation.

Lastly there's *Australia: Journey Through a Timeless Land* with text by Roff Martin Smith and photos by Sam Abell. It's published with *National Geographic*'s imprimatur, and Abell has shot for *National Geographic* for thirty years, so you can expect comprehensive text and excellent photography.

Sometimes the best person to spot the quirks of the natives is an outsider, so here are a couple of books that are written by visitors:

Tony Horwitz hitchhiked around Australia's interior so that we don't have to. *One for the Road: An Outback Adventure* is a very funny description of his journey. He does a terrific job of capturing the relentlessly hot and harsh environment and its often colorful inhabitants. (My favorites were those who measure distances by how many beers they project it will take to reach their destination.) Read this and you'll feel the heat . . . have some of those cold Fosters handy before you start.

The other book of this ilk is Bill Bryson's paean to Australia, *In a Sunburned Country*. He describes his travels in his usual amusing way—witty, self-deprecating, and endlessly curious.

Interspersed among the anecdotes about his own journey, he weaves in facts about poisonous creatures, lengthy earthworms, the hapless early explorers of the outback, and just about anything Australian he uncovers that takes his fancy. (It's such a glowingly affectionate look at the country you can't help but wonder if the bloke has drunk a few too many beers!)

Peter Carey is one of Australia's finest contemporary writers; his novel *Oscar and Lucinda* won the 1988 Booker Prize. Set in the 1800s, it tells the story of two somewhat eccentric characters, minister Oscar Hopkins and heiress Lucinda Leplastrier. They meet on a ship bound for Australia, and are drawn together by their mutual passion for gambling. There's a fragile affection and a foolhardy bet between these two beautifully drawn characters. (You could also cheat and see the movie instead, a pretty good adaptation starring Ralph Fiennes and Cate Blanchett.)

Everyone I've ever met who has visited Sydney has loved it. It's a wonderful, lively city, set on a beautiful harbor, a sparkling place. In the 1990s two well-known and respected travel writers each published a book about it, and try though I may, I could not select one over the other. Geoffrey Moorhouse wrote *Sydney: The Story of a City;* Jan Morris simply entitled her book *Sydney.* Both books mix history with contemporary stories, and both authors skillfully bring their own affectionate impressions of the city to life. If you are fond of Sydney, or if you've ever yearned to go there, toss a coin and pick up one of these books for a good read.

Tim Winton has not yet received the wide acclaim elsewhere that he has in Australia, but I think that it's only a matter of time. I suggest you try his excellent novel *Cloudstreet.* It's set in Perth, the capital of Western Australia, during the postwar years. Misfortune leads two families vastly different in character, the industrious Lambs and the gambling Pickles, to share a large ramshackle house; it's an alliance fraught with problems. Winton describes their lives in beautiful prose filled with warmth and humor. A delight to read.

In early 1788, after an arduous eight-month sea voyage, a sorry collection of prisoners and the military men who served as their jailers disembarked at Sydney Cove—the first white Australians. Because Britain's prisons were overflowing, a new place was needed to dump the surplus criminals, and this was where they chose. These prisoners, many of them charged with nothing worse then petty thievery, were taken away from everything and everybody they'd ever known, transported to the other side of the world, and dropped off at a place the likes of which they'd never seen. The vegetation was hard-leafed and greyish; there were large animals that bounded on two legs and unclad black people with spears; and they'd landed during the Australian summer, which was surely much hotter than anything they'd ever felt in Britain. The disorientation must have been profound and total. If this period of Australia's colonization interests you, there are two books that I recommend.

The first is *The Playmaker* by Thomas Keneally, an expert at creating historical fiction. This book is based on an actual event, the staging in 1789 of a play, performed at the suggestion of the governor to celebrate King George III's birthday. A young Royal Marine, Ralph Clark, was put in charge of finding a cast amongst the prison population, and bringing the performance to fruition. Luckily for us, Clark kept a journal and wrote letters about this endeavor, and from them Thomas Keneally has woven an engaging tale. He writes of Lieutenant Clark's loneliness, yearning for his wife so many thousands of miles away, and attracted to a young prisoner; the challenge of transforming a motley collection of convicts into thespians; and above all he gives a sense of the colony itself, crude and rough, struggling to survive in an inhospitable environment, and almost as much of a prison for the Marines as for the convicts.

The other excellent book on Australia's colonial period is Robert Hughes' *The Fatal Shore.* At more than 600 pages, you may consider it a bit daunting for a weekend, but it is such a fascinating exploration of the time that I would be remiss not to include it. Hughes, well known as the art critic for *Time*

Aussie Rhyming Slang

Australia is well known for its colorful vernacular, and I've always found the rhyming slang to be among the best. It derives from Cockney slang, and is said to have developed as a way to communicate in front of the authorities without them understanding.

It works this way. You replace the one-syllable word that you wish to say with a pair or short group of words, the last one of which rhymes with your base word. Then, to make it especially incomprehensible, you often use only the first word of the replacing words. So if an Australian said to you, "How's it going, china?" he's using the rhyme slang *china plate* for *mate.* Or if you heard "Take a butcher's at this," you need to know that *butcher's hook* is slang for *look.* There are dozens of these expressions, some the same as those used in London, others uniquely Australian, for example, *Reg Grundies* for *undies,* after the name of a famous Australian television game show producer, Reg Grundy. A few more:

after darks / sharks	Jack and Jill / bill
dead horse / sauce (ketchup)	John Dory / story
dog's eye / pie	Oxford scholar / dollar
Germaine Greer / ear	septic tank / yank

I had been wondering if this vernacular was on the decline, until I recently heard, "Give me a couple of Britneys," at a pub. That set my mind at rest.

magazine, spent ten years researching and writing this authoritative tome. He not only details the brutal conditions that the first settlers found themselves in, but also describes the permanent impact that he believes the convict experience has had on Australian society. There's nothing dry about this book; Hughes is a witty and opinionated writer, and if you like a nonfiction book with substance, this is for you.

Movies

Not for everyone, *Love Serenade* (1996) is a deadpan black comedy about a minor radio celebrity, now has-been, who moves into a small town and shakes up the lives of the two sisters next door. They're taken with him, and vie for his attentions . . . although he's so unctuous that it's hard to imagine why. It starts off a little slowly, but you'll slide into the wackiness of it all. And the country town is just too much; it looks godforsaken and ugly in every single scene. No matter where you live, watching this movie will make you grateful that this little fly-spot on the map is not your home.

The Sum of Us (1994) is a chance to see Russell Crowe in a lead role before he became quite so famous. Set in Sydney, it's a sometimes funny, sometimes poignant story of a father and son, both of whom are looking for love, the twist being that the son (Crowe) is gay. The strong bond between the father and son is nicely written, and the Aussie sense of humor is ever present.

In *Over the Hill* (1992) an older American woman, played by Olympia Dukakis, pays an unannounced visit to her daughter in Australia. It does not go well, so in a moment of madness, she buys a souped-up old hot rod and heads off on the open road to see the country. It's your classic road movie. She meets all kinds, has adventures, and finds romance. It's light and fun, with lots of scenery, particularly of the outback, and the Queensland coast.

Strictly Ballroom (1992) is an absolutely delightful little romp, a Cinderella story about a pair of dancers trying to win the major Australian ballroom dancing championships. Paul Mercurio plays Scott Hastings, a talented dancer who wants to dance his own way; he hooks up with Fran, an ugly duckling played by Tara Morice, as his partner. The movie is almost entirely shot indoors, so there are very few clues as to locale, but the quirky quality is Strictly Australian.

Gallipoli (1981) is a gripping story of two young Australian friends who, swept up by patriotic fervor, enlist to fight in World War I and end up fighting at the battle of Gallipoli, one of the greatest military disasters in modern history. The two leads, played by Mel Gibson and Mark Lee, capture the Aussie spirit of the time, exuberant and rough around the edges, and the depiction of their friendship, the "mateship," is wonderful.

My Brilliant Career (1979) is an early film by director Gillian Armstrong, one of a number of period pieces made in Australia in the 1970s. Judy Davis does a wonderful job playing the lead part of Sybylla Melvyn, a spirited young woman from the Australian outback who yearns for a more independent, and more intellectual, life. Not an easy thing to achieve, however, in Australia in the late 1800s. Sybylla's headstrong nature inevitably puts her in conflict with both her family and the social mores of the day, and it's impossible not to feel for her in the struggle. Sam Neill, as her romantic interest, is also excellent. Engaging story line, some pretty rural scenery—you're sure to like it.

Walkabout is director Nicolas Roeg's 1971 story of two British schoolchildren, a teenage girl and her younger brother, who are stranded in the outback. Luckily for them they cross the path of an Aboriginal youth, without whom they would surely perish. The relationship that develops is sensitively shown, and the cinematography of the outback is terrific. There is no better movie for getting a sense of the harshness, and the beauty, of the Australian outback.

Music · · · · · · · · · · · · · · · ·

As an expat-Australian, when I first
heard the strains of "Down Under"
pouring forth from a car radio I had an
instant and visceral reaction—they
were singing about vegemite sand-
wiches and men chundering—this is my song! These are my
people! I was happy. The song by Aussies Men at Work came
from their most popular release, *Business as Usual,* an excellent
1980s pop-rock album with catchy songs and amusing lyrics.
It'll probably make even non-Australians smile.

The best-known Aboriginal band ever, Yothu Yindi, plays an
interesting mix of rock and tribal music, with didgeridoo wonderfully woven throughout. The blend was a smart idea on
their part, as traditional Aboriginal music had never before
found a wide audience. Their album *Tribal Voice* includes the
track that brought them fame, the dance mix of "Treaty," a rock
song about the unhappy relationship between Aboriginals and
the Australian government. Be sure to read the liner notes.

If you're interested in Aboriginal music and are planning
early for your Australian weekend, there's a terrific album you
could order from the Australian Broadcasting Commission: *Culture: Music from Black Australia,* a compilation of various artists

singing in both traditional and modern styles. There's an especially engaging track by the Mills Sisters, who sing "Wadjimbat Matilda," a pidgin English version of "Waltzing Matilda"; it's charming. Order from *http://shop.abc.net.au.*

As is country music in the United States, Australian country is thriving right now, and far and away my favorite artist is Lee Kernaghan. He comes from a country music family (his three siblings perform, and his father won fourteen gold records!) and following in his dad's footsteps, Lee went platinum with his first album. In addition to having a fine voice, Lee sings about life on the land, on the farms, and in the outback, and that's what I like most about him. *The Outback Club* and *Three Chain Road* are my favorites, although they are difficult to find in North America. If you have the time though, they can be ordered at either of these Australian sites: *www.soundworld.hl.com.au* or *www.sanity.com.au.* If that's too slow for you, try *Hat Town,* which is more readily available.

For those a bit more musically serious, I have a few suggestions. Peter Sculthorpe is Australia's best-known orchestral composer. His music is classically based, but influenced by Aboriginal music as well as by music from Indonesia. His work has been included on dozens of albums by artists such as the Kronos Quartet, John Williams, and Pieter Wispelwey, although if you wanted a more comprehensive sample, his album *Sculthorpe: Complete String Quartets Vol. 1* is easily found in North America.

And in the world of opera, Australia has produced two world-famous divas. The first is Dame Nellie Melba (her stage name pays homage to her home city of Melbourne), who from the 1890s into the 1920s was considered the best soprano of her day. She made well over a hundred records, and for those of you interested in early operatic recordings, just a few of those have been released on CD. More recently, Dame Joan Sutherland made her opera debut in England in 1952, and her illustrious career, particularly in the Italian *bel canto* style, earned her the affectionate name "La Stupenda." She has been widely recorded, and you will have no trouble finding her on CD. Her signature role, Lucia di Lammermoor, can be found on *Joan Sutherland: Mad Scenes*.

Food

Australian cuisine, I'm happy to say, has undergone a complete turnaround in the past twenty years. It used to be that most Australians sat down to an evening meal of meat and three vegs—grilled lamb chops perhaps, or a roast, accompanied by some unadorned and quite likely overcooked vegetables. But as the population of Australia has dramatically diversified, so has the food. Thank goodness! Now there is something known somewhat self-importantly as "New Australian Cuisine," which is praised as innovative and vibrant by foodies around the world.

The following cookbooks have all been published in the 1990s, so they all reflect this new culinary reality: *A Taste of Australia: The Bathers Pavilion Cookbook* by Victoria Alexander and Genevieve Harris. The Bathers Pavilion Restaurant is a beautifully situated and popular Sydney eatery. Housed in an historic 1920s building that abuts the sand on Balmoral Beach, it has superb views of the water. The cookbook, with its color photos of the food and the setting, will make you wish that you were there. The recipes reflect the current trend in Australian food, with hints of Mediterranean, French, and Asian influences.

Australia: The Beautiful Cookbook by Elise Pascoe and Cherry Ripe lives up to its name. It alternates recipe chapters with sections on the foods of each of the seven Australian states. The regional pieces are illustrated with gorgeous scenic shots, and with a lot of the food photographed *al fresco,* the book really gives a sense of Australia's varied landscape. It's an absolute pleasure to leaf through, and the recipes are clear and accessible as well.

Australian Food: In Celebration of the New Australian Cuisine, introduced by Alan Saunders, is best for serious foodies. It opens with a lengthy introduction that details the history of food in Australia, before moving into a collection of recipes by chefs and food professionals. Many of the recipes are influenced by Asian and Mediterranean food, yet incorporate Australian ingredients.

For my suggested meal, I am looking backward to a time before the New Australian Cuisine and going for the traditional menu of my childhood. People concerned about their cholesterol will have to seek recipes elsewhere! This meal is one that would be best eaten in winter. If it's summer, I would suggest serving the soup chilled and replacing the roast lamb with a barbecue. Barbecues are tremendously popular in Australia, and none more so than the mixed grill, in which everyone has a lamb chop, a sausage, and half of a piece of steak . . . no fear of meat here.

To accompany the meal there'd be nothing better than a good Australian red. Overwhelmed by the many excellent possibilities, I decided to focus on Shiraz, a variety that Aussie wineries do particularly well. Using the terrific database operated by *Wine Spectator,* I asked for an Australian Shiraz rated as outstanding and costing no more than $20. The four top scorers from that list are as follows: Australian Domain Wines, 1998 Shiraz Barossa Valley Alliance; Peter Lehmann, 1998 Shirz Barossa; Pirramimma, 1997 Shiraz McLaren Vale; Tatachilla,

1998 Shiraz McLaren Vale. (I cannot recommend the *Wine Spectator*'s database highly enough. It includes tasting notes on all listings, and had I chosen a seafood recipe, it would have done just as good a job finding outstanding Chardonnays. See *www.winespectator.com.*)

Fresh Pea Soup

I love the taste of fresh peas, so I think it's worth taking the time to shell them for this recipe. But frozen peas are an acceptable substitute—and will make this recipe much faster!

2 tablespoons butter
1 medium onion, finely chopped
6 cups shelled fresh peas,
or 2 lbs. frozen peas
5 cups chicken stock

½ cup fresh mint leaves, tightly packed,
 plus 4 sprigs reserved
1 cup plain yogurt (can be nonfat)
salt and white pepper to taste

In a large heavy saucepan over medium heat, melt the butter and add the onion. Cook, stirring occasionally, until onion is softened. Add peas and stock and simmer, uncovered, until peas are tender, 5–7 minutes. Stir in mint and remove pan from heat.

Allow soup to come to room temperature, then purée soup in batches in a food processor until very smooth. Add in yogurt and salt and white pepper to taste. Reheat soup over low heat, but do not let boil. Garnish each serving bowl with reserved mint sprig. (If serving soup cold, cover bowl with plastic wrap after puréeing, and chill in the fridge for 3 hours.) Serves 4.

Roast Lamb with Vegetables and Gravy

Serve this dish with steamed green beans and mint sauce for the lamb.

2 large garlic cloves	2 lbs. carrots
1 4-lb. leg of lamb	1 lb. parsnips
2 tablespoons olive oil	2 lbs. onions
3 lbs. potatoes	

For gravy

2 tablespoons all-purpose flour	1 cup water

Preheat oven to 450°F. Peel garlic cloves and cut into slivers. With the tip of a sharp knife, cut 1-inch deep slits all over lamb and insert garlic slivers. Peel vegetables and cut into serving-sized pieces. In a large roasting pan, toss vegetables with olive oil to coat and season with salt and pepper. Bake for 10 minutes.

Reduce oven temperature to 375°F. Push vegetables to the edges of the pan, and place leg of lamb in the middle. Roast lamb and vegetables for 1 hour and 15 minutes or until a meat thermometer inserted into thickest part of meat registers 130°F for medium rare, occasionally loosening vegetables from pan with a metal spatula and turning them, and basting the meat with pan juices.

Transfer lamb to a platter and vegetables to a large bowl and keep warm. To make gravy, pour juices from roasting pan into large glass measuring cup. Deglaze pan with 1 cup of water, then add to juices in measuring cup. Spoon off fat, reserving 2 tablespoons. Heat the 2 tablespoons of reserved fat in the roasting pan over medium-high heat. Add flour; whisk until beginning to color, about 2 minutes. Gradually whisk in pan juices and any juices from lamb platter. Boil gravy until thickened, whisking frequently, about 7 minutes. Season with salt and pepper, and transfer to gravy boat.

Arrange the vegetables on the platter around the lamb and serve with gravy. Serves 4.

Pavlova

See sidebar about how to get passionfruit pulp.

Meringue

4 egg whites   1 cup superfine sugar
pinch of salt   1 teaspoon distilled white vinegar
pinch of cream of tartar   ½ teaspoon vanilla

Filling

¾ cup heavy cream   1 small basket strawberries, washed and halved
½ tablespoon sugar   1 170 g. can (approximately 6 oz.)
½ teaspoon vanilla   passionfruit pulp

Preheat oven to 250°F. Oil a large piece of baking parchment or foil on a baking sheet. In a bowl with an electric mixer at high speed beat the egg whites with salt and cream of tartar until soft peaks form. Gradually add in sugar till stiff peaks form, then beat in vinegar and vanilla.

Spoon the mixture onto the prepared baking sheet into an 8-inch round; use the back of a spoon to make the circle slightly higher around the edge. Cook in the center of the oven for about 1 hour and 10 minutes, until crisp on the outside. Remove paper or foil very carefully (pavlovas can crumble apart), and cool on a rack.

To assemble, whip the cream with the sugar and vanilla into soft peaks, then spread onto the pavlova. Decorate with the strawberries, then pour the passionfruit pulp over the top. Serve immediately so that meringue does not get soggy. Serves 4.

—Jenny Collins

The Aussie Love Affair
with Passionfruit

There is no faster way to add an Australian touch to your desserts than to incorporate passionfruit. Widely grown in Australia, it comes from the passionflower vine (*Passiflora edulis*), so named because the flowers are said to symbolize all of the elements of the passion of Christ. The fruit has a leathery purple-colored exterior, which when sliced open reveals a thick orangey colored liquid in which are suspended black seeds (edible) with a yellow surround. Not the prettiest fruit in the world, but they are delicious.

You can make all kinds of simple desserts with passionfruit: serve slices of pineapple drizzled with passionfruit pulp, or use it as a topping on a dish of vanilla ice cream and sliced bananas, or include it in fruit salads. It also adds a wonderful flavor to crème brûlée or any custard dishes. Because it has a slightly tart citrusy taste, you could also substitute it for lemon in a number of places: cake usually glazed with a simple lemon and sugar syrup would be equally delicious with passionfruit syrup. Or adjust a lemon curd recipe to produce passionfruit curd, which, when added to a tart shell, will make a fabulous tart. Remember though that the canned pulp is sweetened, so you may wish to cut back to taste with the sugar. In some cases you might want to strain out the seeds for the sake of appearance, for example in the crème brûlée and the curd.

If you live in a large metropolitan area, there's a good chance you can find passionfruit pulp, either in cans or frozen, in a specialty food market. If not, you can order it (and many other things Australian) from Australian Catalogue Company, 1 (800) 808-0938, *www.eOZe.net*.

Index

BOOKS

Above Paris (Cameron and Salinger), 65

Adolescent, The (Dostoevsky), 158

Africa Adorned (Fisher), 144

Africa Cookbook, The, 149

African Ceremonies (Beckwith & Fisher), 144

Agony and the Ecstasy, The (Stone), 92

Alexandria Quartet, The (Durrell, L.), 110–111

All the Tea in China (Kit Chow), 204

Altars and Icons: Sacred Spaces in Everyday Life (McMann), 211

Angela's Ashes (McCourt), 52

Aromatherapy Through the Seasons (Bousquet & Fitzsimmons), 169

Arranged Marriage, The (Divakaruni), 174

Art of Brazilian Cookery, The (Botafogo), 12–13

Art of Mexican Cooking, The (Kennedy), 23

Art of Russian Cuisine, The (Volokh), 165

Australia: Journey Through a Timeless Land (Smith & Abell), 247

Australia: The Beautiful Cookbook (Pascoe & Ripe), 243, 258

Australia Wide: A Panoramic View (Duncan), 246

Australian Colors: Images of the Outback (Bachman), 246

Australian Food: In Celebration of the New Australian Cuisine (Saunders), 258–259

Bella Tuscany (Mayes), 89

Bend in the River, A (Naipaul), 145

Bistro Cooking, 82

Brazilian Adventure (Fleming), 7

Brazilians, The (Page), 6

Bronze Horseman, The (Pushkin), 159

Brothers Karamozov, The (Dostoevsky), 158

Café Morocco (Helou), 135

Captain Corelli's Island: Cephallonia (Harris, Terry and Andy), 113

Carnaval (Ancona), 8

China: The Photographs of Lois Conner (Conner), 197

China Chic (Vivienne Tam), 196

China the Beautiful Cookbook (Sinclair), 202

Chinese Kitchens (Yin-Fei Lo), 202

Chinese Way: Healthy Low-Fat Cooking from China's Regions, The (Yin-Fei Lo), 202

Classic Tuscany: The Tuscan Cookbook (Pezzini), 98

Clouds, The (Pushkin), 158

Clouds Should Know Me by Now, The: Buddhist Poet Monks of China, 197

Cloudstreet (Winton), 249

Collected Poems of W.B. Yeats, The (Finneran), 52

Complete Book of Greek Cooking, The (Recipe Club of Saint Paul's Greek Orthodox Church), 118–119

Confessions of a Mask (Mishima), 228

Cooking at the Kasbah: Recipes from My Moroccan Kitchen (Morse), 135

Corelli's Mandolin (De Bernieres), 113

Couscous and Other Good Food from Morocco (Woffert), 135, 136

Cracking the Coconut: Classic Thai Home Cooking (Su-Mei Yu), 216

Crime and Punishment (Dostoevsky), 158

Dagger, The (Pushkin), 158

Dead Meat (Kerr), 160

Delightful Brazilian Cooking (Eng Tie Ang), 12

Devil on the Cross (Ngugi wa Thiong'o), 144

Diary of Frida Kahlo: An Intimate Self-portrait, The, 19

Diego Rivera (Hamill), 19

Dinner with Persephone (Storace), 111

Dispatch from a Cold Country (Cullen), 160

Divine Comedy (Dante), 92

Double, The (Dostoevsky), 158

Dreams of Trespass (Mernissi), 129

Drunken Boat, The (Le Bateau Ivre) (Rimbaud), 72

Dubliners, The (Joyce), 52

Eat Smart in Brazil (Peterson), 12

Elegy for John Donne and Other Poems (Brodsky), 159–160

Eloise in Paris (Thompson), 69

Eloise (Thompson), 69

English Governess at the Siamese Court, The (Leonowens), 213

Epistle to the Prince of Orange (Pushkin), 158

Escape to Morocco (Windo), 129

Essentials of Japanese Cooking, The (Suzuki), 235

Eternal Husband, The (Dostoevsky), 158

Fatal Shore, The (Hughes), 250

Flowers of Evil, The (Les Fleurs du Mal) (Baudelaire), 72

Folk Art of Japanese Country Cooking: A Traditional Diet for Today's World, The (Homma), 235

Food and Wine of Greece, The (Kochilas), 119

Food Lover's Guide to France, The, 82

Food Lover's Guide to Paris, The, 82

Foods of Greece (Kremezi), 118

Foods of India, The (Anand, Brennan & Hutton), 183

Foods of the Greek Islands: Cooking and Culture at the Crossroads of the Mediterranean (Kremezi), 118

France: The Beautiful Cookbook, 82

French Chef Cookbook, The (Child), 82

Galileo's Daughter (Sobel), 89

Gambler, The (Dostoevsky), 158

Germinal (Zola), 71

God of Small Things, The (Roy), 174

Great South Land, The (Duncan), 246

Greece: Land of Light (Gage), 110

Greece from the Air (Arthus-Bertrand), 110

Greek Cuisine (Alexiadou), 119

Greek Vegetarian: More Than 100 Recipes Inspired by the Traditional Dishes and Flavors of Greece (Kochilas), 119

Healthy Latin Cooking Cookbook (Raichlen), 12

Henri Cartier-Bresson: Mexican Notebooks (Cartier-Bresson & Fuentes), 18

Heritage of Scotland: A Cultural History of Scotland and Its People (Harris), 34–35

He's Leaving Home: My Young Son Becomes a Zen Monk (Miura), 229–230

Hideous Kinky (Freud), 130

House of Niccolo (Dunnett), 35

I Have Lived to Bury My Desires (Pushkin), 158

Idiot, The (Dostoevsky), 158

Images of Japan: Japan the Four Seasons (Hymas), 228

In a Sunburned Country (Bryson), 247–248

In Tuscany (Mayes), 90

Interpreter of Maladies (Lahiri), 174

Invitation to Indian Cooking, An (Jaffrey), 182–183

Irish Heritage Cookbook, The (Johnson), 57

Irish Proverbs, 51

Irish Traditional Cooking (Allen), 57

Italian Farmhouse Cookbook (Loomis), 98

Izu Dancer and Other Stories, The (Kawabata), 228–229

Jacques Pépin's Simple and Healthy Cooking, 82

Japanese Kitchen: 250 Recipes in a Traditional Spirit, The (Tsai), 235

Jasmine (Muhkerjee), 173

Latin American Art (Sullivan), 6

Le Divorce (Johnson), 68

Less Than One (Brodsky), 160

Like Water for Chocolate (Esquivel), 19

Linnea in Monet's Garden, 69, 71

Log from the Sea of Cortez (Steinbeck), 19–20

Long Ago and Not So Long Ago (Jadis et Naguère) (Verlaine), 72

Lover, The (L'amant) (Duras), 71

Lymond Chronicles (Dunnett), 35

Maasai (Ole Saitoti & Beckwith), 144

Madame Bovary (Flaubert), 71

Madeline (Bemelmans), 68

Magus, The (Fowles), 113–114

Mammy, The (O'Carroll), 52

Mandarins, The (Les Mandarins) (de Beauvoir), 71

Maroc (Watson), 128

Master of Petersburg, The (Coetzee), 160

Mastering the Art of French Cooking (Child), 82

Me Talk Pretty One Day (Sedaris), 67

Memoirs of a Geisha (Golden), 230

Memoirs of the Dead (Dostoevsky), 158

Mexican Sayings: The Treasure of a People (Ballesteros), 20

Michael Jackson's Complete Guide to Single Malt Scotch: The Connoisseur's Guide to the Single Malt Whiskies of Scotland, 45

Michelangelo: The Poems (Ryan), 91–92

Mistress of Spices, The (Divakaruni), 174

Modern Greek Poetry (Frair), 111–112

Moor's Last Sigh (Rushdie), 174

Morocco: Sahara to the Sea (Cross), 128

Morocco Modern (Ypma), 128

Most Beautiful Villages of Greece, The (Ottaway), 110

Most Beautiful Villages of Tuscany, The (Bently), 90

Mother Ireland (O'Brien), 52

Moveable Feast, A (Hemingway), 66

My Family and Other Animals (Durrell, G.), 110

No Exit (Huis Clos) (Sartre), 71

Notes from the Underground (Dostoevsky), 158

Odyssey (Homer), 112

Old Gringo, The (Fuentes), 19

Olive Grove: Travels in Greece, The (Kizilos), 111

On Mexican Time (Cohan), 18–19

One for the Road: An Outback Adventure (Horwitz), 247

Oscar and Lucinda (Carey), 248

Paddy Clarke Ha Ha Ha (Doyle), 53

Paris to the Moon: Essays on Contemporary Paris (Gopnik), 65–66

Part of Speech, A (Brodsky), 160

Personal Matter, A (Oe), 229

Petersburg (Bely), 159

Playmaker, The (Keneally), 250

Poems Without a Hero and Selected Poems (Akhmatova), 159

Portrait of Scotland (Baxter), 35

Possessed, The (Dostoevsky), 158

Prospero's Cell: A Guide to the Landscape and Manners of the Island of Corcyra (Durrell, L.), 111

Provence: The Beautiful Cookbook, 82

Real Thai: The Best of Thailand's Regional Cooking (McDermott), 216

Recipe of Memory: Five Generations of Mexican Cooking (Kennedy), 23

Red Azalea (Anchee Min), 196

Red Balloon, The (Lamorisse), 73

Robert Burns: Selected Poems, 35

Sacred Space: Clearing and Enhancing the Energy of Your Home (Linn), 211–212

Sailor Who Fell from Grace with the Sea (Mishima), 228

Samba (Guillermoprieto), 7

Sand Child, The (Tahar Ben Jalloun), 129

Satanic Verses, The (Rushdie), 174

Savory Scottish Recipes (McDonald), 41

Scottish Fairy Tales, 35

Serengeti: Natural Order on the African Plain (Iwago), 142

Sheltering Sky, The (Bowles), 129–130

Simply Thai Cooking (Young), *217*

Sister of My Heart (Divakaruni), 174

Snow Country (Kawabata), 229

Sound of the Mountains, The (Kawabata), 229

Spectacular Australia (Matthews), 247

Spring Moon (Lord), 197

Stones of Florence, The (McCarthy), 90

Stranger, The (Létranger) (Camus), 71

Suitable Boy, A (Seth), 173

Sydney: The Story of a City (Moorhouse), 248–249

Sydney (Morris), 248–249

Tale of Genji, The (Murasaki Shikibu), 228

Taste of Australia: The Bathers Pavilion Cookbook, A (Alexander & Harris), 258

Taste of Mexico (Quintana), 23

Thai Massage: A Traditional Medical Technique (Gold), 213

Thai Massage Manual: Natural Therapy for Flexibility, Relaxation and Energy Balance (Mercati), 213

Thai Style (Warren), 212–213

Thailand: The Golden Kingdom (Warren), 212–213

Things Fall Apart (Achebe), 144

Timeless Places: Greek Isles (Brooks), 110

Traveler's Tales: Brazil (Haddock & Dogett), 6

Tropical Asian Style (Tettoni), 212

True Thai: The Modern Art of Thai Cooking (Sodsook), 217

Tuscan Childhood, A (Beevor), 90

Tuscan Year: Life and Food in an Italian Valley, The (Romer), 91, 98

Tuscany: Authentic Recipes from the Provinces of Tuscany (de Medici), 98

Uffizi: Florence, 89

Under the Tuscan Sun: At Home in Italy (Mayes), 89

Under the Volcano (Lowry), 20

Urania, To (Brodsky), 160

Vita Nuova (Dante), 92

Waiting (Ha Jin), 197

War in the Val d'Oricia (Origo), 92

Weep Not Child (Ngugi wa Thiong'o), 144

Within Tuscany: Reflections on a Time and Place (Spender), 90

Words of 101 Irish Songs and Ballads, The, 51

World Vegetarian (Jaffrey), 135

Would-be Gentleman, The (Le Bourgeois Gentilhomme) (Moliére), 71

Year in Provence, A (Mayle), 70

Years with Laura Díaz, The (Fuentes), 19

Zorba the Greek (Kazantzakis), 112–113

MOVIES

African Queen, The, 147

An American in Paris, 75

Angela's Ashes, 54

Anna and the King, 214

Anna Karenina, 162

Aparajito, 176

Arabian Nights, 131

Backstage at the Kirov, 162

Bandit Queen, 176

Barroco, 21

Beach, The, 214, 215

Bossa Nova, 9

Braveheart, 38

Breaking the Waves, 38

Bullet in the Head, 200

Burnt by the Sun, 162–163

Bwana Devil, 147

Casablanca, 130–131

Central Station, 8–9

Cinema Paradiso, 94

Cleopatra, 131

Commitments, The, 53

Crime Story, 200

Crouching Tiger, Hidden Dragon, 200

Desperado, 20

Dry White Season, A, 147

Dubliners, The, 54

Eat, Drink, Man, Woman, 199

El Mariachi, 20

Emperor and the Assassin, The, 198

Farewell My Concubine, 198

4 Days in September, 9

Gallipoli, 253–254

Gandhi, 175

Ghost and the Darkness, The, 147

Gladiator, 131

Gods Must Be Crazy, The, 147

Gojira, 231

Hamlet, 163

Hard-Boiled, 200

"Hermitage Masterpieces" (video series),
    160–161

Heroes Shed No Tears, 200

*Hiroshima, Mon Amour (Hiroshima, My
    Love),* 74–75

Idiot, The, 161–162

Il Ciclone, 95

Iphigenia, 114–115

Jean de Florette, 76

Jewel of the Nile, 131

Jules et Jim (Jules and Jim), 74

Kagemusha, 230, 231

Kama Sutra, 176

Killer, The, 200

King and I, The, 214, 215

King Lear, 163

La Gloire de Mon Père (My Father's Glory),
    76

Land of Smiles: Thailand, 214

Last Emperor, The, 198

Last Temptation of Christ, The, 131

Lawrence of Arabia, 132

*Le Château de Ma Mère (My Mother's Cas-
    tle),* 76

Legend of Drunken Master, 200

*Les Enfants du Paradis (Children of Par-
    adise),* 73

*Les Parapluies de Cherbourg (The Umbrel-
    las of Cherbourg),* 73–74

Life Is Beautiful (La Vita e Bella), 95

Like Water for Chocolate, 20

*Living Edens: Thailand: Jewel of the Ori-
    ent, The,* 214

Lord of the Flies, 214

Love Serenade, 252

Manon des Sources (Manon of the Spring),
    76

Mask of Zorro, The, 20
Mediterraneo, 115
Michael Collins, 53–54
Mishima: A Life in Four Chapters, 230
Mogambo, 146
Morocco, 131
Mummy, The, 131
Mummy Returns, The, 131
My Brilliant Career, 254
*National Geographic's Africa Animal
    Oasis,* 146
Never on Sunday, 114
Night of the Shooting Stars, The, 93
Old Gringo, The, 20
Once a Thief, 200
Operation Condor, 200
Oscar and Lucinda, 248
Out of Africa, 146
Over the Hill, 253
Passage to India, A, 175–176
Pather Panchali, 176
Pillow Book, The, 231–232
Princess Mononoke, 231
Raise the Red Lantern, 199
Ran, 230–231
Rashomon, 230, 231
Red Balloon, The, 72–73
Red Dust, 146
Rise and Fall of Idi Amin, The, 147
Rob Roy, 38
Romola, 93
Room with a View, A, 93–94
Rumble in the Bronx, 200
Secret of Roan Inish, The, 53
Shirley Valentine, 115

Spies Like Us, 131
Strictly Ballroom, 253
Sum of Us, The, 253
Supercop, 200
Tea with Mussolini, 95
The Wedding Banquet, 199
Titanic, 214
Tokyo Story, 230
Trainspotting, 38–39
Tschaikovsky, 162
Up at the Villa, 95–96
Video Visits China (travelogue), 198
Waking Ned Devine, 54
Walkabout, 254
Woman in the Dunes, 231
World of Apu, The, 176
Xiu Xiu: The Sent Down Girl, 199
Yellow Earth, 199
Yellow Ticket, The, 161
Zorba the Greek, 115

MUSIC

All the Best from India, 179
"Amore o grillo" *(Madama Butterfly)*
    (Puccini), 97
*Ancient-Contemporary Music from Thai-
    land* (Fong Naam), 215
*Anoka: Soundz from the Asian Under-
    ground* (Singh), 179
*Anthologie de la melodie russa et sovie-
    tique,* 163
Arie Sacre (Bocelli), 97
Auld Lang Syne, 36–37

Berber: Music from the High Atlas Mountains (various artists), 133

Best Ever Scottish Compilation, The, 39

Best of Boccherini, The (Boccherini), 97

Best of Mano Negra, The (Negra), 78–79

Best of the Chieftains, The, 56

Boccherini: The Guitar Quintets (Boccherini), 97

Bombay the Hard Way, 179

Boris Gudenov (Mussorgsky), 164

Brasil: A Century of Song, 11

Business as Usual (Men at Work), 255

Cello Concerto #2, 3, 9, 10 (Boccherini), 97

"Che gelida manina" *(La Bohème)* (Puccini), 97

China Meditation, 201

Classical Music of Northern Thailand, 215

Culture: Music from Black Australia, 255–256

Days Long Ago (Burns), 36–37

Di Efchen (Alexiou), 117

Dreaming of You (Selena), 21

Each Little Thing (Shannon), 56

Edith Piaf: Her Greatest Recordings, 77

En Vivo (Maná), 21

Enchanted Forest-Melodies of Japan, The (Galaway), 232

Fiddler's Dance, The (Scottish Fiddle Orchestra), 39

Fifth Book of Madrigals (Monteverde), 96

Firebird Suite, The (L'oiseau de feu) (Stravinsky), 164

Flute and Sitar Music of India: Meditational Ragas, 177

Gharnati: Arabo-Andulusian Music of Morocco (Alaoui), 132

Gianni Schicchi (Puccini), 97

Greek Fire (Annabouboula), 118

Greek Folk Favorites (Panegyris), 116

Hat Town (Kernaghan), 256

If You're Feeling Sinister (Belle & Sebastian), 39–40

In Concert (Burke), 56

India's Master Musician (Shankar), 179

Into Africa, 148

Irish Tenors, The, 56

J'ai Deux Amours: Mon Pays et Paris (I Have Two Loves: My Country and Paris) (Baker), 77

Japan: Traditional Vocal and Instrumental Music, 232

Je Te Dis Vous (Kaas), 78

Jilala: Sufi Trance Music From Morocco (Bowles & Gysin), 133

Joan Sutherland: Mad Scenes (Sutherland), 257

Jungle Talk: The Natural Sounds of the Wilderness, 148

Khovanshchina (Mussorgsky), 164

Kismet (Borodin), 164

La Bohème (Puccini), 97

L'Incoronazione de Poppea (Monteverde), 96

Luige Boccherini: 28 Symphonies (Boccherini), 97

Madama Butterfly (Puccini), 97

Man Who, The (Travis), 39–40

Masterpieces of Chinese Traditional Music, 201

Mediterranea: Songs of the Mediterranean (Yannatou), 117

Mexican Revolution, The, 21

Mexico's Greatest Hits (Los Capacaba), 21

Min'yo: Folk Songs from Japan (Yujiro), 232

Mourmourike: Songs of the Greek Underworld, 116

Music from the Court of St. Petersburg (Vol. II), 163

Music From Uganda 1 & 2, 148

Music of Hikari Oe (Oe), 233

Music of Kenya and Tanzania, The, 148

Musica Popular Brasiliera (MPB), 11

"Nessun Dorma" *(Turandot)* (Puccini), 97

Nights in Tuscany (Bocelli), 97

Once Upon a Time in China: The Best of Chinese film Music, 201

100 Años de Mariachi, 21

Out the Gap (Shannon), 56

Outback Club, The (Kernaghan), 256

Paris My Love, 78

Per Amore (Bocelli), 97

Phases of the Moon: Traditional Chinese Music, 201

Pictures at an Exhibition (Mussorgsky), 164

Portrait, A (Dalaras), 117

Prince Igor (Borodin), 164

Prose Compat (MC Solaar), 79

Puccini, Giacomo, 96–97

"Recondita armonia" *(Tosca)* (Puccini), 97

Rite of Spring, The (Le sacre du printemps) (Stravinsky), 164

Romanza (Bocelli), 97

Rough Guide: The Music of Japan, 233

Sabil' A Salaam (Marrakech), 132

Scheherazade (Rimsky-Korsakov), 164

Sculthorpe: Complete String Quartets Vol. 1 (Sculthorpe), 256–257

"Si Mi Chiamano" *(La Bohème)* (Puccini), 97

Sogno (Bocelli), 97

Sounds of India, The (Shankar), 179

Symphony #2 in B minor (Borodin), 164

Symphony #1 in E-flat minor (Borodin), 164

Tex-Mex, 21

Thailande-Thailand: Ko Samui, 215

Three Chain Road (Kernaghan), 256

Tosca (Puccini), 97

Tribal Voice (Yothu Yindi), 255

Turandot (Puccini), 97

"Un bel di" *(Madama Butterfly)* (Puccini), 97

Very Best of Mikis Theodorakis, The (Theodorakis), 117

Waltzing Matilda, 244–245

When Irish Eyes Are Smiling, 55, 56

Witchcraft & Ritual Music: Kenya & Tanzania, 148

Zorba the Greek (Theodorakis), 117

RECIPIES

Aloo Baigan Sabji, 185-186

Ants climbing trees (spicy noodles), 206

asparagus, over toasted brioche, 84–85

Avogolemono soup, 121

Baklava, 123–124
beans
   and fish stew, 151
   mealie, 150
   white, in tomato sauce, 102
beef, See meats
bell pepper and tomato salad, 138
berry ice, 30
beverages
   caipirinha, 13
   hot chocolate, Mexican, 31
   lassi, 188
   margaritas, 30
   Moroccan mint tea, 126–127
   Whiskey Toddy, 44
Blinchikis Povidlom, 168
Bombay Beef with Curry Butter, 186
Borsht, Kholodnyi, 165, 167
bread, brown, 58–59
Brioche aux Asperges, 84–85
butter, curry, 186
cabbage, curried, 152
cachaca, 13
Caipirinha, 13
cake, Dundee, 43–44
carrot salad, 138
chicken
   fajitas, 28–29
   poached, 167–168
   yellow curry sauce, 220–221
   chicken-coconut soup, 219–220
chili salt, 27
chocolate mousse, 85
corn on the cob, grilled, 152

couscous with lemon, chicken and
   olives, 136–137
curry
   butter, 186
   eggplant and potatoes, 185–186
   yellow with chicken, 220–221
dahl, 184–185
Daikon Pickle, 236
desserts
   baklava, 123–124
   chocolate mousse, 85
   dundee cake, 43–44
   hot oatmeal apple crumble, 60
   kheer, 187
   mungunza, 16
   pancakes, 168–169
   pavlova, 262
   shortbread, 41
dundee cake, 43–44
eggplant, curried with potatoes, 185–186
Fagioli all'uccellotto, 102
fajitas, chicken, 28–29
fish broth, Dashi, 236
fish stew and beans, 151
Frittata de Cipollo, 99–100
Gaeng Garee Gai, 220–221
gazpacho, Mexican, 28
guacamole, 27
Hjiki, 236
hominy, 16
hot chocolate, 31
kheer, 187
Kuritsa Otvarnaia, 167–168
lamb, with vegetables, 261

lamb kebabs, 122–123
lassi, 188
Maize Mealie, 151
margaritas, 30
meats
   beef, tangerine, 205
   bombay beef with curry butter, 186
   roast lamb with vegetables and gravy,
     261
meringue, 262
Minestrone di verdura, 100
miso soup, 237
Moqueca de Camaroa, 15
Moroccan mint tea, 126–127
Moules à la Marinière, 84
Mousse au Chocolat, 85
Mungunza (hominy dessert), 16
mussels, in white wine sauce, 84
noodles
   ants climbing trees (spicy), 206
   shirataki, 237–238
   soba, 238
oatmeal apple crumble, 60
onion frittata, 99–100
orange, date and almond salad, 137
oranges and flower petals, 222
pavlova, 262
pea soup, 260
peanut stew, 153
Phad Priawan Phak, 221–222
Pollo at Diavolo, 101–102
Pomodori Fritti, 99
Potatoes, curried, 185–186
Potato soup, 58

rice, Mexican, 29–30
Rumbledethumps, 43
Salade Nicoise, 83
salads
   bell pepper and tomato, 138
   carrot, 138
   Nicoise, 83
   orange, date and almond, 137
   spinach with sesame seeds, 235
   tomato and yogurt (Tamatar Raita),
     187
salsa, 25
salt, chili, 23, 27
Samosas, 183–184
sauces
   dipping, Thai, 218–219
   tomato, 101
   white wine, with mussels, 84
   yellow curry, 220
seafood
   Moqueca de Camaroa, 15
   mussels, in white wine sauce, 84
Shepherd's Pie, 42
shirataki noodles, 237–238
shortbread, 41
soba noodles, 238–239
soups
   Avogolemono, 121
   beet, cold (borsht), 165, 167
   chicken-coconut, 219–220
   dahl, 184–185
   fresh pea, 260
   hot and sour, 203
   Mexican gazpacho, 28

Minestrone di verdura, 100
miso, 237
potato, 58
Spaghetti al Salsa di Pomodoro Crudo
(spaghetti with tomato sauce), 101
spinach salad with sesame seeds, 235
spinach with garlic, 207
spring rolls, vegetarian, 218–219
stews
beans and fish, 151
Moqueca de Camaroa, 15
peanut, 153
spicy meat, 150
Sukiyaki, 237–238
sweet and sour vegetables, 221–222
Tamatar Raita, 187
Tangerine beef, 205

tea, Moroccan mint, 126–127
Tom Kha Gai, 219–220
tomatoes, fried, 99
vegetables
asparagus over toasted brioche, 84
cabbage, curried, 152
corn on the cob, grilled, 152
curried eggplant and potatoes,
185–186
daikon radish, 236
kale, cooked, 16
onion frittata, 99–100
spinach with garlic, 207
sweet and sour, 221–222
tomatoes, fried, 99
Whiskey Toddy, 44
Zaru Soba, 238

To Our Readers

CONARI PRESS publishes books on topics ranging from spirituality, personal growth, and relationships to women's issues, parenting, and social issues. Our mission is to publish quality books that will make a difference in people's lives—how we feel about ourselves and how we relate to one another. We value integrity, compassion, and receptivity, both in the books we publish and in the way we do business.

As a member of the community, we donate our damaged books to nonprofit organizations, dedicate a portion of our proceeds from certain books to charitable causes, and continually look for new ways to use natural resources as wisely as possible.

Our readers are our most important resource, and we value your input, suggestions, and ideas about what you would like to see published. Please feel free to contact us, to request our latest book catalog, or to be added to our mailing list.

Conari Press
2550 Ninth Street, Suite 101
Berkeley, California 94710-2551
800-685-9595 • 510-649-7175
fax: 510-649-7190 • e-mail: conari@conari.com
www.conari.com